T0350092

Stay Safe!

A Basic Guide to Information Technology Security

ABDUL B. SUBHANI

abbott press

Abbott Press books may be ordered through booksellers or by contacting:

Abbott Press
1663 Liberty Drive
Bloomington, IN 47403
www.abbottpress.com
Phone: 1 (866) 697-5310

ISBN: 978-1-4582-2027-1 (sc)
ISBN: 978-1-4582-2028-8 (hc)
ISBN: 978-1-4582-2029-5 (e)

Library of Congress Control Number: 2016910680

Print information available on the last page.

Abbott Press rev. date: 7/15/2016

To my parents

Special contributions by

Dr. Faisal Amjad
&
Sarah Untalan

Edited by
Christopher Walton

Contents

CHAPTER

Introduction to Security

Defining Security

What is security?

Is it a state of well-being for systems, organizations, or people? Can it be achieved through safety from criminal activity, such as terrorism, theft, or espionage? Does it include procedures followed or measures taken to ensure feelings of safety, stability, and freedom from fear or anxiety?

Security is all of these things and more. Specifically, in computer systems, security is expressed as the system's degree of resistance to, or protection from, harm.

Foundations of Security

Security is built on the following foundations:

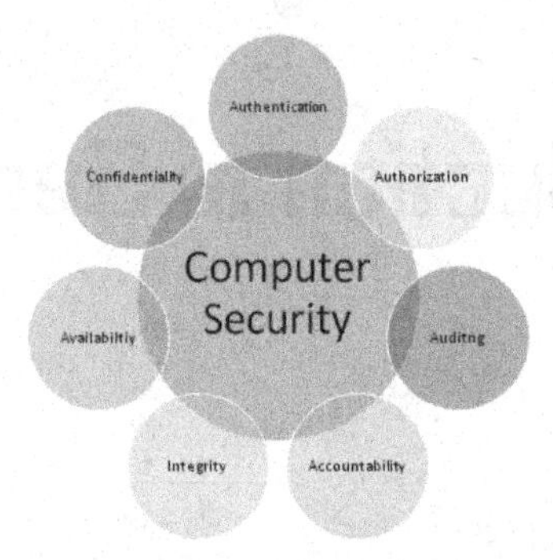

Figure 1.1: Computer security foundations

Authentication

Put simply, authentication is the process of verifying the identity of a person or thing. It might involve confirming the identity of a person by validating identity documents, verifying the validity of a website with a digital certificate, tracing the age of an artifact by carbon dating, or ensuring that a product is what its packaging and labeling claim it is. Authentication often involves verifying the validity of at least one form of identification.

Authorization

Authorization is the function of specifying access rights to resources. More formally, *to authorize* is to define an access policy based on roles and permissions.

It is easy to confuse authentication with authorization. The two are frequently used interchangeably in conversation and are often tightly associated as key pieces of a secure system. But the two are very different concepts. Authentication is the process by which an individual's identity is confirmed. Authorization is the association of that identity with rights and permissions.

Auditing

Auditing is normally used as a finance-related term. However, in the realm of security, auditing is an unbiased examination and evaluation of an organization's security goals. It can be done internally (by employees of the organization) or externally (by an outside firm).

Confidentiality

Confidentiality involves a set of rules or a promise that limits access or places restrictions on certain types of information. In day-to-day life, people do not share all of their personal information with every person around. Information is shared on a need-to-know basis or it is protected, according to the requirements of its holder. All of this falls under the foundation of confidentiality.

Integrity

The commonly understood meaning of integrity is the quality of being honest, having strong moral principles, and sometimes, the state of being whole and undivided. In security, integrity is further defined as the state of a system performing its intended functions without being degraded or impaired by changes or disruptions in its internal or external environments.

Availability

In secure systems, availability is the degree to which a secured system resource, such as a system, a subsystem, or equipment, is in a specified operational and accessible state at the start of a task, when the task is called for at an unknown or random time.

Availability is linked to other security foundations as well. The availability of a resource to those accessing it should be according to their roles, permissions, and authorization.

Accountability

One goal of computer security is that anyone with access to a secured system should be held accountable for his or her actions within the system. For example, if a document has been amended by person X, and if later X denies having amended it, the system should be able to hold X accountable by showing evidence that the document was amended by X.

Security Terminology

When discussing security, it is important to be aware of these frequently used terms:

- **Assurance**: A guarantee or level of guarantee that a secure system will behave as expected when put to use.
- **Risk**: A possibility that something may go wrong. While working to make a system secure, one must consider the risks to the security.
- **Threat**: A method of triggering risk. Any action needed to make a system secure is based on preventing the threats posed to the system.
- **Vulnerability**: A weakness in a system that can be exploited by a security threat.
- **Countermeasures**: Ways and means to stop a threat from triggering a risk.
- **Exploits**: Vulnerabilities that have been triggered by a threat.

Different Kinds of Security

After becoming familiar with basic security terminology, the next stage is to understand the different types of computer security.

Internet security

Internet security is a set of rules and actions meant to protect against online attacks. The Internet has become part of our daily lives—a basic need for individuals, organizations, and systems. Internet security works to ensure confidentiality by protecting access to authorized resources and services. One example is an online system that prevents credit card details from being stolen on a shopping website.

Information security

Information security means defending information from attempts by unauthorized entities to use, disclose, disrupt, modify, peruse, inspect, record, or destroy a system. *Information* is a generic term for any form of data, whether physical or electronic.

Mobile security

Mobile security, as the name suggests, is the security of mobile devices like smartphones, tablets, laptops, and other portable computing devices. Because this type of security also includes securing the networks that mobile devices use to operate, it is sometimes referred to as wireless security.[1]

---

[1] Mobile security is examined and discussed in much greater depth in chapter 16.

Network security

Network security is a specialized field involving securing a computer or mobile network infrastructure against threats. Network security includes the policies and procedures implemented by a network administrator or manager to avoid and keep track of unauthorized access, modification, exploitation, or denial of the network and network resources.

CHAPTER

Introduction to Computer Security

What is Computer Security?

Computer security is designed to protect computer systems from theft or damage to the software, the hardware, and the information on them, as well as from disruption or usurpation of the services they provide.

Computer security has the following three major security objectives, based on several of the previously discussed security foundations:

- Confidentiality: Disclosure of information is on a need-to-know basis or per roles and permissions.
- Integrity: Data can be altered in authorized ways by authorized users only.
- Availability: Data should be accessible to those authorized to access it.

Why is Computer Security Important?

Prevention against data theft is essential. So much data, such as personal information, credit card information, bank account numbers, passwords, and work-related documents, is stored in computers used by people on a daily basis. Not securing a computer against breaches can lead to data becoming compromised by unauthorized and malicious parties.

Malicious intent can pose a vital threat to the security of a computer. An intruder can alter program source codes and use personal pictures or email accounts to create derogatory content, such as pornographic images or fake, misleading, and offensive social media accounts. Vengeful people might crash computer systems to cause data loss. Intruders may hack other computers, websites, or networks and then use them in denial-of-service or similar attacks to prevent access to other websites and servers.

It is important to keep data safe, secure, and confidential. This is only possible by understanding the threats to our computer systems, being aware of possible countermeasures, and paying necessary attention to the subject of computer security.

Types of Computer Security Threats

The computer security life cycle begins with ascertaining the threat environment. One can correctly guard systems only against known threats. Therefore, it is important to take note of the different types of threats posed to computer systems.

Malware[2]

Malware is any malicious program or software designed to perform harmful or unwanted actions on a computer system. Some malware attacks computer applications and data, while other malware steal confidential data from systems. It is important to note that *malicious intent* is a requirement in deeming a code malware. Unintentional

[2] Malware is explored in greater detail in Chapter 5.

flaws, such as bugs or run-time errors, cannot be defined as malware. Typical types of malware include computer viruses, worms, Trojan horses, spyware, rootkits, and backdoors.

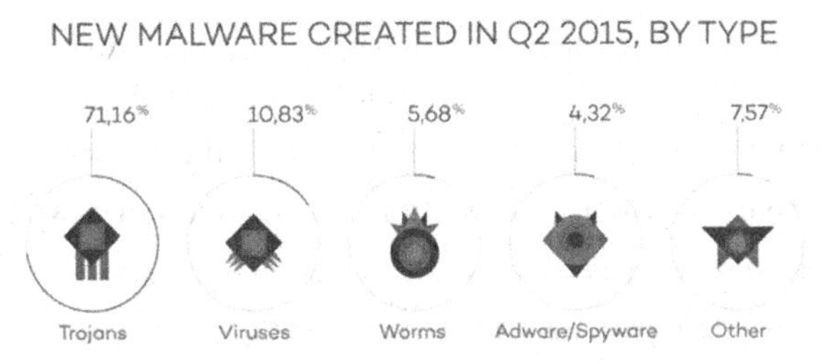

Figure 2.1: New malware created in the second quarter of 2015[3]

Grayware

It is important to talk about grayware while describing computer security threats. Grayware is a term coined for applications that are unwanted, annoying, and troublesome but cannot be termed malware. Grayware may degrade a system, but not as much as malware. It includes adware, fraudulent dialers, hoaxes, software bundlers, browser modifiers, some types of spyware, and more. Typical grayware activities include capturing keystrokes, bombarding a system with ads, stealing data, installing unwanted software, playing pranks or false warnings, modifying system settings, and modifying functionality.

Computer Security Best Practices

With so many different types of malware and grayware, computer systems require specific security measures to combat the dangerous threat environment. Although this book aims to explain all threats,

[3] Panda Security, *Panda Labs Report*, Q2 2015.

vulnerabilities, and related defensive mechanisms and practices, this section looks at the best practices for computer security.

Use an antivirus program[4]

In today's threat environment, use of an antivirus program is vital for protecting a computer's normal functioning capabilities. A good antivirus is usually bundled with Internet security, anti-spyware, and anti-adware features. Antivirus vendors keep making protection mechanisms for upcoming malware; therefore, antivirus programs must always be updated with new virus definitions.

Keep software updated

In addition to the operating system's core system software, which performs the computer system's primary tasks, computers use a host of application software for routine tasks, such as documentation, programming, watching movies, and web surfing. A system can be compromised through a vulnerability in any of the software, whether it is the system software or the application software.

Many times, software vendors identify a vulnerability in their software and then create and release patches in the form of software updates. These updates are offered through notifications to the clients who are already using the software. This aspect becomes much more important when the software is an antivirus program. Antivirus updates are new virus definitions. If an antivirus program is not updated with the new definitions, it will not be able to guard against the latest known malware.

When a vulnerability has been identified and an update has been released, the vulnerability becomes public. It is not very hard for attackers to exploit such known vulnerabilities, since half of

---

[4] Antivirus software is discussed in greater depth in chapter 6.

their job—identifying the vulnerability—has already been done. Therefore, all users who do not update their software immediately after release of a patch are highly vulnerable to attacks. In summary, computer users should never delay in installing a security update.

Take care in installing new software

First and foremost, only install software when it is absolutely necessary. When there is a need to install new software, either through external media, like disks, or directly downloaded from Internet, make sure that the software is from a trusted source. If the software is downloaded directly, it should be obtained from the official website of that software.

Avoid pirated and cracked software at all costs. It is not very difficult to get allegedly free software (*freeware*) from peer-to-peer sites, but money saved in this way will very likely be wasted—along with much more money spent fixing the system later. Never underestimate the cost of hassle and trouble of losing data.

Utilize user account controls

Current operating systems provide elaborate user account controls for better system management. This feature is also useful in securing a system efficiently. There should not be any default accounts without a password. No one should be using the root or superuser account routinely. Routine and normal working users should not have permissions to install/uninstall software or change system settings. That creates less chance of compromising the system accidentally by a naïve user installing harmful software.

Use firewall software[5]

Firewall software protects the system against unauthorized connections and traffic. This keeps the system protected from malware exploits unknowingly installed by harmful sites and software. Basic firewall software is typically bundled with the operating system. It is often easy to configure and works reasonably well in default configuration.

Be extremely cautious in giving out personal information

In the modern-day threat environment, one has to be careful about giving out personal information. Phishing and social engineering attacks are common ways of getting or stealing personal information from people around the world.[6]

Use password protection

The importance of password protection cannot be overemphasized. Weak passwords, reusing passwords, custody/security of passwords, password leakage, etc. are part of the big issue of password protection.

People tend to use simple passwords that they can remember easily. Sometimes, with the same intentions, people reuse passwords with different websites and systems. But a reused password only makes the person more vulnerable. Attackers can use an email or username at one site along with the associated password from another site or system to gain access to both.

---

[5] Firewalls are discussed in much greater depth in Chapter 9.

[6] These topics are defined and discussed in much greater depth in Chapter 15.

Best password practices include:

- Not reusing passwords for multiple websites and systems
- Keeping complex passwords with a variety of alphanumeric characters
- Not sharing passwords
- Not writing passwords down in obvious places

Minimize storage of sensitive data

A good way to remain secure is to not store any passwords. If that is not possible, minimize the location and the amount of sensitive data that is stored to make it easier to store in a safe place. If storing sensitive data electronically, use a removable media or tertiary storage; if writing it down in a journal or other book, make sure the document hidden from plain view while at the computer system.

Remember physical security[7]

Last, but not least, on the list of best practices is physical security. Other security measures are rendered useless if the hardware is stolen. Physical security is less important for desktop computers and large servers, but it is more important for portable hardware like laptops, mobiles, removable media, etc. Keep electronic devices all under lock and key or with you while traveling or moving around.

[7] Physical security is discussed in greater depth in Chapter 14.

CHAPTER

Access Control

What is Access Control?

Access control is the set of legitimate procedures to access a system. A person, a device, or a service, such as an application program or a web service, may want access to a system to use a service, read or write data, or utilize a resource. Simply put, access control can be understood as mechanisms for guarding entry to a system, similar to people implementing security in the form of guards, a photo ID verification system, keys, etc. to grant access to their property.

A good access control system should deny entry to unauthorized and malicious parties while allowing admission to legitimate users. It should have elaborate methods for adding to and excluding members from a list of allowed users. Its administrative procedures should be concise and comprehensive to avoid mistakes and ambiguity.

Subject and object in access control

Understanding the details of access control requires understanding the distinction between subject and object. The *subject* wants access to some information, resource, service, or application. The *object* is the information, resource, service, or application being accessed.

For example, if a user tries to open a file, then the user is the subject and file is an object. Whether the user will be allowed to open the file is a question of access rights. The entity or system with the power to grant access has the access control of that particular file.

Classification of Access Control

In the computer security world, access control is classified based on the controlling authority that decides the access permission of an object. There are four basic classifications of access control:

- Mandatory Access Control (MAC)
- Discretionary Access Control (DAC)
- Originator Controlled Access Control (ORCON or ORGCON)
- Role Based Access Control (RBAC)

Mandatory access control (MAC)

Mandatory access control (*MAC*) is when access to a system is controlled by the system's own mechanisms/tools. As the emphasis is on the rules and regulations of the system, which are not easily changed by the user, mandatory access control is also called *Rule Based Access Control.*

The access control mechanisms built into operating systems are examples of MAC; neither the subject accessing the system nor the objects being accessed by that subject have any role in determining grant of access. Usually, the operating system's routines themselves grant access based on the attributes associated with the subject needing access and the object being accessed.

Discretionary access control (DAC)

Discretionary access control (*DAC*) is when an individual user can set the access control rights and permissions of an object. As this type of access control is linked to the identity of individual users, it is also called *Identity Based Access Control (IBAC)*.

Here, the individuality or the identity of the user or application that owns an object at a particular time holds prime importance. The owner has the right to decide who is allowed and who is denied access.

An example of DAC is a personal diary. The author of the diary has complete control. The author may not allow anyone access, allow a significant other to read it, or publish it for all to read. DAC is totally at the discretion of an object's owner.

Originator-controlled access control (ORCON/ORGCON)

In this case, the access control is set by the creator or the originator of an object. With computers, this means the file originator decides the access rights of other subjects regarding that file.

For example, processor-manufacturing company A contracts micro-coding company B to develop a new micro-coding language for its new product—a microprocessor for high-end embedded systems. In order for B to design such a language for A's microprocessor, B needs a copy of A's microprocessor design. A gives the copy of its microprocessor design to B, but adds a clause in the contract binding B to not share the design without A's prior permission. This is a typical scenario where ORCON can be very important. Here, B may be in possession of the microprocessor design as owner of the information, but it still cannot set access control for anybody else without the consent of A, the originator/creator of that design.

Role-based access control (RBAC)

This type of access control is a slightly varied form of MAC. In *Role Based Access Control* (*RBAC*), access control for a particular object lies with a subject holding a specific role. The access control rights lie with the specific role, rather than with the particular subject. In RBAC systems, the ability or requirement to access some data, service, or application depends on the subject's job description:

> Jane Doe is a clerk in the accounts management department of an organization. She is responsible for assisting the accounting director in managing various accounts. Due to the nature of her job, she has access to details of the organization's various accounts. After some time, Jane is transferred to the human resources department (HR) of the same organization. Due to her change in role, she no longer has access to the organization's account details, but she does have access to the company's HR-related information. A new person employed as the accounts clerk would now have access rights to the accounts.

Jane's story is an example of access rights to a particular object or set of objects based on appointments or roles. Furthermore, an individual in possession of more than one role would have access rights as per the job description of each of the roles.

Examples of access control classification

To gain a better understanding of access control classification as discussed above, Table 3.1 lists some examples.

Example	Type of Access Control
Default file permissions in an operating system	Mandatory Access Control
An office where no report can be distributed without the CEO's consent	Originator Access Control

A government facility where only ministers can enter	Mandatory Access Control
A hospital, in which a doctor can see the records of a particular patient, provided that the patient has given permission for the doctor to see them	Discretionary Access Control

Table 3.1: Examples of access-control classifications

Steps of Access Control

The study of access control would be incomplete without revisiting the differences between three of the security foundations discussed in the first chapter: identification, authentication, and authorization. These interrelated concepts have subtle but important differences, especially when considered in the context of access control.

Identification

When a subject tries to access an object, an access control entity or system will confirm the subject's identity to check for access rights regarding that particular object. The subject proves its identity in the form of a user name, process ID, ID card, or other credentials that uniquely identify the subject in that system.

Authentication

Authentication proves that the form of identification offered by the subject is linked to that particular subject. Approval or rejection occurs after the subject presents its identity in the form of some credentials.

The process of authentication or establishing identity includes one or more of following:

- What is known to the subject? (i.e., a password or a pass phrase)
- What is possessed by the subject? (i.e., some token, badge, photo ID, or smart card)
- What is the subject? (i.e., biometrics of the subject, such as fingerprints, retina scan, or facial recognition methods)
- What is the location of the subject? (i.e., where the subject is with respect to the system, such a specific door, terminal, or computer system)

A typical authentication system includes:

- Authentication information
- Complementary information associated with the authentication information stored on the system
- A complementation system to convert authentication into complementary information
- An authentication function to decide on approval or rejection
- Functions for creating and making changes to the authentication information

Authorization

No subject can have any authorization without first being identified and authenticated. On the other hand, a subject who is authenticated is not necessarily authorized to perform every function within a system.

For example, no one can enter your house without offering evidence (identification) proving identity (authentication). But just because someone is authenticated to enter your home, that does not mean they are also authorized to drive your car.

In access control principles, authorization includes the *principle of least permissions*, meaning that people should only be authorized to perform actions absolutely necessary for completing assigned duties. If the starting permissions are too small, additional permissions may be added later. On the other hand, it would be a poor approach to first authorize subjects with all possible permissions and then later withdraw permissions that are unnecessary.

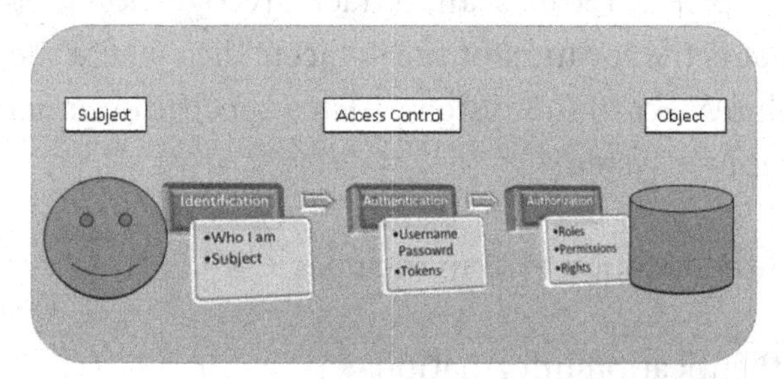

Figure 3.1: Steps of access control

CHAPTER

Application and Web Security

What is Web Application Security?

Most computer systems today are connected in the massive, global, network of networks known as the *Internet*. Information that travels over the Internet does so via a variety of languages known as *protocols*.

HTTP, perhaps the most well-known protocol, is the language used by the information superhighway known as the *World Wide Web*. The Web includes many different servers, which support *web pages*—documents written in a special format called *hypertext markup language* (*HTML*). Users access these web pages through web browser software installed on their computer systems.

While accessing web pages, it is possible to access unwanted material that can harm a computer system. Users often access software through web applications hosted on web pages. Like normal computer applications, web applications may hide malicious code that can cause damage to users' computers.

Web application security can be thought of as a branch of information security or computer security dealing with the security of information systems on the World Wide Web. Reliance on the Web is ever-increasing and so are the related threats. Some of the most common current threats are cross-site scripting, SQL injection attacks, denial of service (DoS), cross-site forgery, arbitrary code execution, and phishing.

Users access web pages through browsing software by typing in the *Uniform Resource Locator* (*URL*) of the servers that host the pages. Before going into the details of web application security threats and vulnerabilities, let us first consider some of the actions users might perform while browsing the Web.

- Viewing contents of a web page
- Clicking on a link and opening a new page
- Searching through a search engine
- Filling out a form
- Using an e-commerce website to make a purchase
- Creating or signing in to an online account
- Downloading software or data, such as media files

Risks Associated with Web Applications

For many individuals, and even some organizations, web security is not an issue until a breach through some web application service occurs. However, as mentioned above, as reliance on the Web increases, so do the associated risks and level of threat.

Cross-site scripting (XSS)

Cross-site scripting (*XSS*) enables attackers to inject client-side script into web pages or web applications to run malicious code. Understanding XSS requires an understanding of client-side script and same-origin policy.

Client-side script is code to be executed on the client side, as opposed to the creator side (*backend*), in the web browser. XSS is a vulnerability normally exploited by attackers to bypass access controls like same-origin policy.

Under *same-origin policy,* web browsers allow code contained in an initial web page to access data in another web page, if both pages originated from the same secured connection. Such a policy stops malicious codes on one web page from gaining access to data on linked pages.

XSS is not a direct attack against a particular user. Rather, it exploits a vulnerability in a web page visited by the user to pass malicious code to the user's web browser. XSS especially takes advantage of software and scripts such as JavaScript, VBScript, ActiveX, and Flash.

To target a specific user, an attacker may use social engineering techniques to persuade the user to visit an infected page. For the attack to succeed, the infected website requires user input on that particular web page. Then the attacker can insert code in the payload sent to the user's browser. When the payload reaches the user's browser, the attacker's code executes without the user's knowledge.

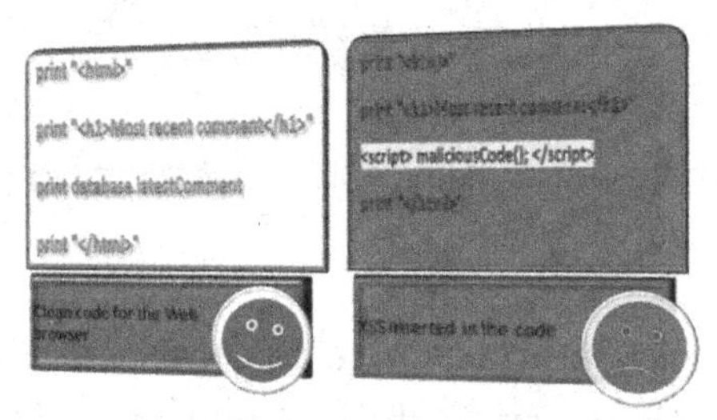

Figure: 4.1: Cross-site scripting (XSS)

SQL injection

SQL injection vulnerability is one of the oldest, most widespread, and most hazardous of all web application vulnerabilities, as it can affect any website or web application with a back-end database written in a special database language called *structured query language (SQL).*

In SQL injection, an attacker executes harmful SQL statements (malicious payloads) to take over the SQL database server behind a web application. It is even possible for attackers to effectively bypass a web application's authentication and authorization mechanisms and retrieve the entire content of the underlying database. At minimum, the attacker could then easily add, delete, or modify the contents of the database.

SQL injection can be used to steal sensitive data stored by a website, such as user credentials, credit card data, personally identifiable information (PII), commerce secrets, or trade secrets.

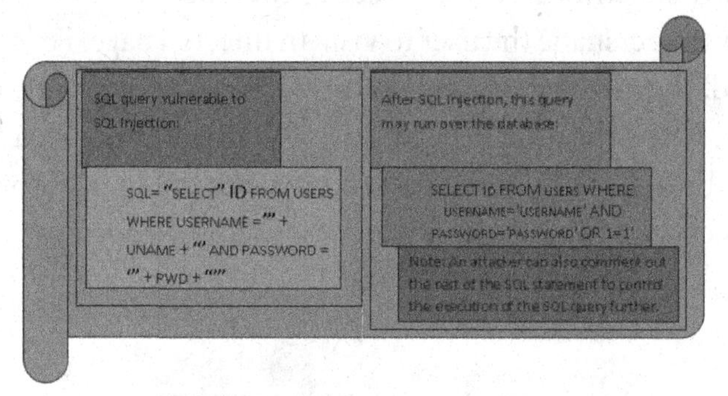

Figure 4.2: SQL injection methodology

To execute an attack, the attacker has to gain access to an application that is part of an SQL query. At the moment a website gets user input and includes it in its SQL query, an attacker can insert malicious code. The malicious code then becomes part of the legitimate query to be run on a database.

Understanding the potential damage of an SQL injection attack requires understanding the use of SQL for a database or *relational database management system (RDBMS)*. SQL can be used for viewing data, but it can also be used to modify and delete data. In some cases, an RDBMS can also execute commands on an operating system. Therefore, a successful SQL injection attack can do any of following:

- Bypass authentication or impersonate a target user
- Completely disclose data
- Cancel transactions, modify balances, etc. leading to serious data integrity and non-repudiation violations
- Destroy data, leading to wide-scale non-availability
- Attack an internal network behind the firewall, if the database allows execution of operating system commands

Cross-site request forgery (CSRF)

In a *cross-site request forgery* (*CSRF*) attack, the user's web browser is tricked so that its authorization to access a website is abused. In other words, an attacker deceives a client browser to misuse its credentials or access rights to assist in the attacker's malicious designs.

The impact of such an attack varies according to the user's authorization and the sensitivity (or dollar value) of the data available through the website being accessed by the user. If the CSRF target is an administrator, the complete web application under attack is threatened. Other examples of malicious activities include stealing credit card data, performing a transfer of funds, and submitting a form with fake information via the user's browser without the user ever knowing.

For example, bank account holder X is logged into the bank's legal website through a legitimate user account. While X is accessing the bank's web services, a session is established with the bank's web server. A *web session* is the log of activities performed by a user, identified by an IP address, on a website. To track a session, web browsers keep small files called *cookies* on the user's machine. At this time, attacker Y, making use of the established session, manipulates

X's browser to do something malicious on Y's behalf—in this case, steal X's money.

Suppose X uses the URL *http://somebank.com/app/transferFunds?amount=aaa&destination*

Acct=bbbb to engage in the session with the bank's web application. Y creates another web page with the content:

<img src="http://somebank.com/app/transferFunds?amount=aaa&destinationAcct=bbbb" width="0" height="0" />

Using this malicious web page, X's browser tries to collect an image at the above-mentioned link, but this transfers funds from X's account to Y's account, which the bank's web server takes as a legitimate command.

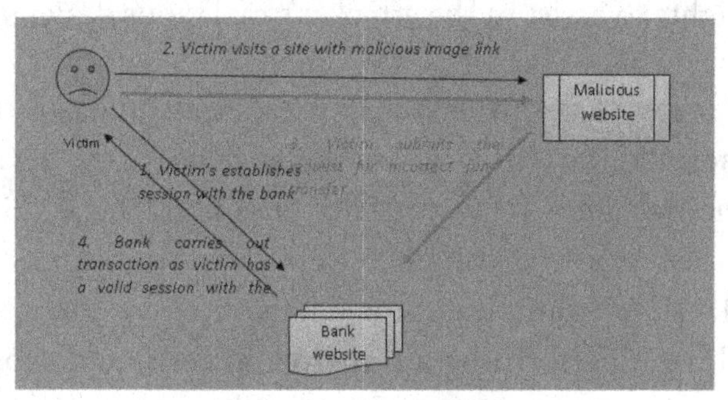

Figure 4.3: Cross-site scripting forgery

Improving Application Security by Avoiding Misconfigurations

Generally, web applications face more security threats than do applications deployed on isolated systems or on small networks. This is mainly because the larger user base of a web application generates more possible threat scenarios. With such large user bases, the threats to web applications due to incorrect configuration and faulty coding can prove disastrous. Some of the common mistakes related to websites and web applications are described below.

Injection flaws

As mentioned above, in the case of SQL injection and XSS, attackers insert attack commands into the SQL server or the client browser, respectively. This leads to data loss, hijacking, and many other problems.

This exploit is available to the attacker as a result of failing to filter untrusted or unwanted input. Untrusted input (from untrusted sources or of a malicious pattern) must not be permitted to reach the back end. This means the input to the web application must pass through some filtering mechanism, such as a whitelist[8]. The filtering mechanism should be flawless; one out of a thousand inputs bypassing the filtering mechanism could cause irreparable damage.

Broken authentication

Multiple bugs or errors can result in faulty authentication. However, their causes may be different, such as:

- Session ID is exposed
- Session IDs is easily guessable
- Passwords of users stored in *clear* (unencrypted) or not protected in transit
- Session timeouts not handled properly

To avoid such bugs in the code, utilize time-tested frameworks instead of attempting to re-invent the wheel.

---

[8] Discussed in further detail in Chapter 6.

HTML injection vulnerability

Another misconfiguration that can make a website or application vulnerable to injection attacks is returning *HTML tags*—snippets of text that are hard-coded in the back end—to the users. Such a vulnerability may lead to injection of plain HTML content. The effect of such an attack may not be devastating, but it can be annoying. A simple, preventive measure against HTML injection is to not return HTML tags to the user side.

Insecure direct object references

When an internal object, such as a database key or some file, is accessible to the client, it is defined as a *direct object reference*. An attacker can incorrectly be allowed authorization by providing the necessary direct object reference for gaining access. Insecure direct object reference exposure to users typically occurs either due to false trust in all users or back-end complacency.

Password resetting

Normally, websites or applications give users the ability to reset their passwords. However, an attacker might use this ability to reset the password of a privileged user, such as *admin* or *administrator*. It is important to consistently and correctly authorize users for such important tasks.

Sensitive data exposure

With only a little bit of carelessness, a misconfiguration can expose sensitive data to the client side. Sensitive data should always be encrypted both in storage and in transit, and, if it is no longer required, it should be disposed of as soon as possible. For example, keeping customers' credit card data is a serious responsibility that, if handled carelessly, could bring huge losses in terms of cost and reputation.

Also, no sensitive data should travel in cookies or in URLs. The preferred safeguard for data transit is to use only secure channels, like HTTPs (a secured version of the Web-standard HTTP protocol), or *virtual private networks (VPNs)*. Cookies should have a secure flag.

Lack of level access control

At times, some web developers mistakenly think that client-side users cannot access the server's access control and authorization functionalities since they are not accessible through the user interface. However, as discussed above, attackers can forge requests to access such functionalities.

For example, an attacker may access a button, available only on the administrator panel of a server page, to perform some administrative tasks or to gain further privilege for doing malicious acts. This is possible when authorization is not properly configured for such areas, due to a false sense of security. In order to avoid such lapses, proper authorization mechanisms must be ensured.

Using components with known vulnerabilities

While developing a web application, developers may take shortcuts by using freeware tools or by reusing code for interfaces. This is a common practice, but it requires caution. Reusing code and using freeware might seem very convenient but comes with security risks. On the other hand, paid software has vulnerabilities that must be patched with vendors' regular updates. Before inserting off-the-shelf code, a developer must evaluate and analyze it for *bugs* (misconfigured code) and *backdoors* (malware which provide unauthorized entry into a system). Moreover, it is important to realize that development does not end with the launch of the web application or website; there must be occasional audits and testing for various scenarios.

Invalidated redirects and forwards

This is another case of faulty filtering of inputs at a website or application. An attacker can insert code into an HTTP header and make redirects to malicious sites and harmful downloads without users' knowledge. For example, if a site has a redirect link with the GET parameter for taking a URL, the attacker can manipulate the parameter to create a URL to a malicious site, but the user may consider the redirect safe. The easiest way to prevent these kinds of attacks is to not keep redirect links or to create a fixed list of trusted locations.

Other misconfigurations

There is no end to the list of misconfigurations or code flaws that can lead to attacks because there is no lack of ways and means to damage. Additional methods include:

- Enabling the debug option while running the application
- Enabling directory listing on the server
- Running unnecessary services
- Keeping default passwords or keeping them unchanged for a long period of time
- Revealing stack traces to an attacker

CHAPTER

Malware

What is Malware?

As was briefly discussed in Chapter 2, malicious software, otherwise known as malware, is a prime threat source for computer systems. Malware can cause minor, harmless disturbances or complete destruction. These software programs are written to cause harm by changing the functionality of a system or part of a system and taking advantages of vulnerabilities, or, at times, creating new vulnerabilities.

Malware must be differentiated from bugs and errors. Bugs and errors are software flaws that occur due to developers' unintentional mistakes; malware is created with malicious intent. This chapter digs deeper into the categories and logic of malware.

What Might Change in the Infected System?

The effects of malware can vary vastly, from subtle to devastating, depending on the type and freedom of action available to the malicious software. Possible effects are discussed below.

System settings changed

Changes to system settings may be minor in the beginning, like changing a browser's *home page* (the first page it automatically visits upon opening) or adding a toolbar or a new icon in the *system tray* (typically located in the bottom right corner of the screen). Some changes may be even more subtle, but they must be addressed, as they could be the start of system infection.

Slowed system response

An infection can slow a single application or even a whole system down to a crawl. Sometimes, the slowness is due to some other issue, such as network problems or simultaneously running too many applications. However, if the slowness is constant, the system is likely infected with malware. A closer look at the system's task manager may reveal suspicious programs running that were not initiated by anyone.

Too many pop-up ads

Encountering lots of pop-up ads while on the Internet is another sign of an infected system. Pop-ups may vary from harmless advertising to warnings of system infections or data deletion.

Unintended file changes

An alarming indicator of the presence of malware on a system is unintended changes in file names or extensions. These may be hidden, system, or user files. Sometimes old files go missing or new files are created without any user action. These all are signs that the system is likely badly infected and requires immediate action to remedy the issue.

System startup failure

An even more alarming effect of malware can be a system startup failure. The computer system may become unable to open user programs and perform basic system functions. Sometimes startup issues are a result of user activity, such as incorrect changes in system startup configurations, incorrect installation of application software, or a hardware failure, such as failure of the hard disk drive, etc. However, with a little investigation, a user can discover whether a startup issue is a result of user activity or something else. Either way, the system would require a thorough overhaul.

Abrupt system crashes or shutdowns

Another upsetting indicator of malware's presence can be abrupt system crashes or unscheduled shutdowns. At first, the only problem may be an inability to run user applications or system services. However, such problems should be taken seriously, even if they do not happen on a regular basis. Users should determine the last changes made or last running program when such crashes occur. Sometimes the problem is not malware; instead, it might be a result of hardware issues or an incorrectly installed/configured program.

Denial of certain user actions

Cases of denial of certain actions by users can indicate the presence of malware. For example, emails sent from a user account without the account owner's knowledge, files deleted, or configuration changes made.

Disabled or uninstalled services without user interaction

Disabling of system services, uninstalling of applications without user action, and deactivation of antivirus software or a firewall are clear signs of an infected system, requiring quick action. Such severe indicators show an impending system crash.

Misbehaving system

Malware is the likely cause if a system starts generally misbehaving, such as opening unintended programs, redirecting to web pages not asked for, or clicking an icon and opening an unintended file or program.

Asymptomatic

Even when there is no trace of anything unwanted, a system may be infected by malware. Malware are designed to go undetected until the damage intended is complete, and they can go undetected for a long period of time.

Different Types of Malicious Software

Malware can be categorized based on their way of working, design architecture, and area of influence. Common categories of malware include viruses, worms, Trojans, adware, spyware, and rootkits.

Virus

Similar to biological viruses, which infect a cell and then reproduce to spread the infection, a computer *virus* traditionally refers to an executable program that replicates itself and inserts its copies into other programs and data on the same computer system and on other networked computer systems. It may utilize system functions or other programs to reproduce quickly.

However, for the purpose of differentiating viruses from other malware, it is important to note that viruses do not execute themselves. Instead, they are dependent on other programs for execution.

Viruses can be considered the beginning of malware, but nowadays, there are hardly any new viruses around. Viruses have mostly been replaced by successors, such as worms and Trojan horses. Since some of these successors technically can be considered variants of viruses, the scope of the term *virus* has been widened to refer to an entire family of malware.

Worm

Worms resemble viruses—with a significant difference. Although the terms are often used interchangeably, viruses, by definition, need another program to execute and replicate. By contrast, worms are more devastating than viruses because they can replicate themselves without the aid of another program.

Worms carry all the code and functionality necessary to perform their intended malicious tasks and replicate without the use of other programs. Worms replicate rapidly and are specially designed to use the Internet or other networks to spread. A worm may also include other types of malware, such as a Trojan horse, as its payload. Some of the most notorious outbreaks of malware have been worms.

Trojan horses

The *Trojan horse*, often simply referred to as a *Trojan*, is any malware that pretends to be a harmless utility program but actually has a malicious intent and application. Its name is taken from the trick used by the Greeks against the Trojans in Virgil's *Aeneid*. A Trojan may masquerade as a useful/legitimate program, or it may actually perform a useful task as a cover for a clandestine, malicious one, such as making the victim machine a member of a botnet community, discussed below.[9] Traditionally, and by definition, Trojans do not self-replicate. However, Trojans are often combined with worms to guarantee their self-replication.[10] Trojans can reach a system through USB flash drives, downloads from untrusted and harmful websites, and e-mail attachments.

Key loggers are special Trojans that record keyboard strokes and/or mouse activity on the system and pass on this information to the owner of the malware, to cause further damage. They are used to record personal information, such as passwords, credit card data, and more. The actual harm then occurs in the forms of stolen data, impersonations, and fraudulent purchases.

Key loggers can be further divided into the following classes:

- *Kernel-based* key loggers reside in the operating system and intercept, record, and pass on key strokes that pass through the kernel.[11] Such key loggers are difficult to code and hard to detect. They may be considered part of the device driver for the keyboard because, in this case, keystrokes from all programs would eventually fall prey to the key logger.
- *API-based* key loggers attach to the keyboard API of a running application, capture keystrokes, and store the information for further action.
- *Form-targeting* key loggers attach themselves to the "submit" button at the end of a form and record the form data before it is sent to the legitimate recipient.
- *Memory injection-based* key loggers make changes to the memory associated with web browsers in order to bypass an operating system's access control mechanisms.

---

[9] *See* **Zombie computer**, below.

[10] *See* **Worms**, above.

[11] The *kernel* is the central component of most computer operating systems—a bridge between applications and the actual data processing done at the hardware level.

- *Packet analyzers* search unencrypted network traffic to retrieve passwords.
- *Remote access software* key loggers reside on a computer system, record keyboard strokes, and send data to some remote location.
- *Hypervisor-based* key loggers settle themselves into the hypervisor, below the operating system, and behave like virtual machines.[12]

Adware

Adware are programs that act as catalysts to display ads on a computer system based on usage statistics.

Not all adware is malware. Some adware collect user data, with the user's consent, in order to guide the user to specific areas of interest. These adware are legitimate programs that cannot be defined as malicious.

However, other, malicious, adware programs can be installed onto users' systems without their consent; these adware programs then collect user data. They also affect web usage in order to direct the user to unintended websites and can bombard users with so many ads that normal browsing becomes difficult, if not impossible. Such adware are said to display Trojan-like behavior.

Adware, like most other malware, typically does not make its presence obvious. A normal user may not detect any trace of adware on the hard drive or any indication of program installation on the system.

The malicious adware may be a *software bundler*, unknowingly installed along with freeware so the providers can get revenue by sending usage statistics to merchants for targeted ads. Alternatively,

[12] Also called a virtual machine manager, a *hypervisor* is a program that allows multiple operating systems to share a single hardware host.

the adware may be a *browser hijacker*, acquired by an intentional or unintentional visit to a malicious website where the system is penetrated through browser vulnerabilities.

Spyware

Spyware is normally coupled with the malicious adware programs as discussed in the previous section. Spyware, as the name indicates, spies on the user and collects data about usage patterns. Usage patterns include the sites the user visits and the location where the user normally accesses the Internet. This information can reveal the user's current and related interest areas. Usage patterns make it easy for adware to show users ads relevant to their interests, which has proven to be a productive marketing strategy for merchants.

Spyware functions similarly to adware, but it is usually a separate program. However, like adware, it is installed unknowingly either while another freeware program is being installed or during access to malicious websites.

Apart from helping adware, spyware can also be used to collect information about email addresses, passwords, and credit card data.

Rootkit

A *rootkit* is a devastating type of malware that resides in the *root*—the lowest level of the operating system. *Operating systems* manage services, hardware, file systems, etc., illustrating the access that rootkits can acquire and explaining how rootkits still go undetected by many antivirus programs. Rootkits, even if detected, are difficult to remove and require special methods.

Once it is in a system, a rootkit can allow other malware to install and run without being detected, create fake user accounts, and even capture and pass on data, including keyboard strokes.

Zombie computers

Rootkits and their payloads (malware the rootkit allows to operate undetected) are generally used by attackers to create a backdoor for access to steal data, falsify documents, conceal other malware, such as key loggers or viruses, or force the victim machine to become a zombie computer.

A *zombie computer* can be employed by an attacker to send attack commands or codes to other systems on a network. Zombie computers become part of a larger set of such hacked systems, called a *botnet*, used in unison by the attacker or handler to launch denial of service (DoS) attacks, click frauds, and other types of malicious activities.

In a typical distributed DoS attack though a botnet, the attacker takes control of multiple systems using covert malware, such as a Trojan, to implant malicious code. Once a sufficient number of computers are part of the botnet, the attacker sends attack commands to the botnet through an open port. The attack command makes each of the zombie computers in the botnet send a huge amount of data to the target website, overwhelming the handling capacity of the website's servers and making the site unable to service its legitimate users.[13]

Drive-by download

While not explicitly a type of malware, a *drive-by download* occurs when a user visits a website and malware unknowingly downloads to the user's computer without any links being clicked. This malware strategy normally exploits an application or add-on in the client-side of a browser or a security vulnerability in an outdated operating system. The initial download is often so small that the user does not even notice. The only job of the initial code is to contact another

[13] DoS attacks are described in greater detail in Chapter 8.

system from where it can download the rest of the malware onto the user's machine.

Scareware

Scareware, once installed on a system or encountered on the web, scares users and tricks them into doing or buying something that they otherwise would not. One example is a pop-up that claims the computer system is infected and its data is about to be corrupted but then offers to disinfect the system if the user pays some amount of money or clicks a link that will covertly install a Trojan horse on the system. Scareware can come from a drive-by-download or from a web page that has other malicious code embedded in its script.

Ransomware

Similar to scareware, *ransomware* first modifies targeted files on the hard drive, just enough to make them unusable, before offering some sort of solution for a cost. After taking the user's money, the attacker just resets the file data back to normal. An example of ransomware is the attacker encrypting headers of important files, maybe system files or some critical data, and then decrypting the headers into their original form to make them useable again after receiving payment.

Malware Attack Steps

After understanding the different types of malware, it is important to understand how a malware attack actually happens. Typically, a malware attack infects a computer system in five steps.

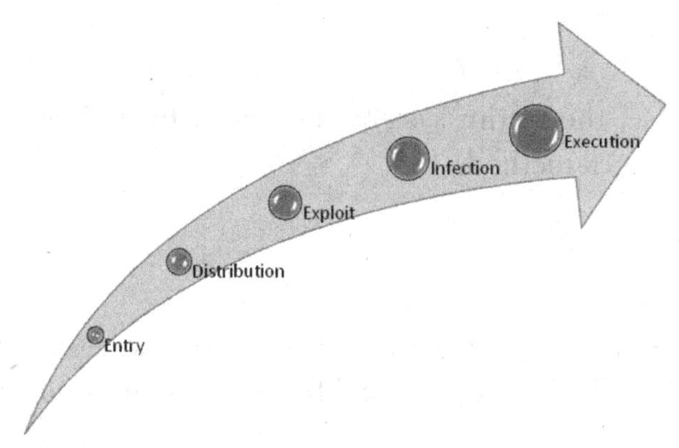

Figure 5.1: Steps in malware attacks

Entry

Entry is the initial contact of malware with the victim computer system, such as when the system's browser opens a malicious website or freeware is downloaded to the system. Normally, this piece of the malware that first enters the computer system is harmless until it spreads around the system, bringing in related malware from a remote site or attacker, and then carries out its intended malicious activity.

Distribution

The initial malware code, which was tiny and harmless, comes in contact with its remote master, sometimes by directing the victim system to the malicious site, and begins replicating, usually covertly and unnoticed. The initial malware code might also collect basic data, such as operating system type, operating system version, and system resources, and send this data to the remote malicious system to ensure that subsequent malware is compatible.

Exploit

In this phase, the victim system is checked for vulnerabilities to determine attack methods.

Infection

The malware, specific to the victim system and its particular vulnerabilities, is downloaded, and the user system is infected.

Execution

In this last step, the downloaded malicious code is executed. As discussed above, the amount of damage is determined through the design and category of the malware.

Malware Development Motive

After understanding malware and the damage it can do, many people ask "who is making malware, and why?"

The simple and straightforward motive behind almost all malware development is money. Criminals make malware to take money in different ways, as nearly all malware can lead to some form of financial benefit to its perpetrator. Examples include:

- Impersonating someone to open fake accounts
- Stealing credit card data to use in fraud
- Extorting ransom money
- Selling a cure for some infections (possibly nonexistent or manufactured)
- Forcing a user to buy specific piece of hardware or software

CHAPTER

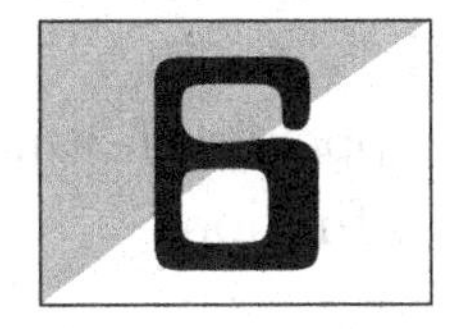

Antivirus Software

What is Antivirus Software?

The purpose of *antivirus software* seems apparent from the name. Initially, antivirus software were developed to guard against computer viruses. But, as discussed in the previous chapter, viruses were only the first malware tools created. Therefore, today's antivirus software not only guard against viruses; they also work to avert, search for, identify, and eliminate other malware, including worms, Trojans, rootkits, and spyware/adware. This software is expected to include basic functionalities, such as:

- Scanning the complete system, specific files/folders, or specific areas to detect malware, flag it, and then quarantine it or remove it altogether
- An option for users to configure scheduled automatic scans of the complete system or part of the system
- Scanning a specific file before it is opened by the user
- *Live protection*—a constant, active guard against any new malware or malicious activity
- Appropriate mechanisms, such as quarantine or removal, to stop malware, once detected, from damaging the system without incapacitating the system

- Tracking the health of the system and showing the status to the user on demand
- A mechanism and supporting features for staying up-to-date with new malware definitions

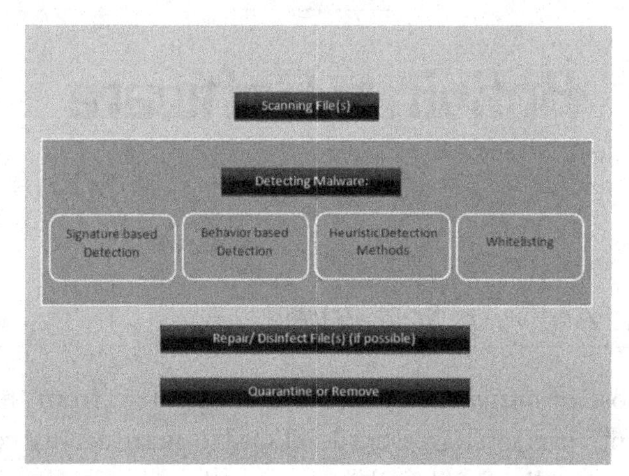

Figure 6.1: How antivirus software work

Methods to Identify Malware

While antivirus software must provide a range of functionality to keep a host system secure and well-guarded against malware attacks, the first and foremost functionality remains malware detection. It is the malware-detection feature that distinguishes a good antivirus program from a bad one. The reason is simple and obvious: all other functionalities are dependent on the detection of malware. Without virus-detection capabilities, the other functionalities will be useless.

However, while malware detection is important, it is also the most difficult task for antivirus software to perform. New malware constantly appear, and new malware formulation techniques are always emerging. Antivirus software depend on a live-protection feature to remain active and relevant regarding new threats.

Malware detection includes updating and releasing guards against new malware threats. In order to update itself with new malware definitions, antivirus software must have a reasonable mechanism for detecting new and upcoming malware. Antivirus software use one or more of a variety of methods to accomplish this task.

Signature-based detection

Signature-based detection can be considered essential for antivirus software. Antivirus software includes a database of all malware signatures that it has ever encountered and detected. Using signature-based detection, when an antivirus program checks a file for threats, it compares the contents of the file with the dictionary of malware signatures in its database.

What is a *malware signature* (or *virus signature*)? It is a malware's malicious code. If the content of the scanned file matches a malware signature in the antivirus software's signature database, the antivirus declares it a malware and recommends further action, from isolating or repairing the file to complete removal of the file, depending on the nature of threat.

Because new malware is released daily, signature-based detection requires continuous updates of the malware signature database. The malware signature database can be updated based on research by antivirus software vendors or reports of new threats by users.

Signature-based detection is very effective and quick when it encounters malware already listed in the malware signature database. However, malware authors wishing to fool this method can succeed with only a little extra effort. Oligomorphic, polymorphic, and metamorphic malware coding methods allow malware to encrypt their own parts or simply modify themselves as a method of disguise, so as to avoid a match in the malware signature dictionary.

Behavior-based detection

Signature-based detection requires the antivirus software to use a predefined, but regularly updated, database of known malware signatures and compare it with files being scanned. However, smart malware programmers try to dodge this static, signature-detection method by coding the malware in a way that changes its signature.

Antivirus vendors, as a countermeasure to such malware coding techniques, use behavior-based methods to detect malware. For example, a burglar who is planning to break into a house may first do some preparation, such as using surveillance to gain information about the house, its surroundings, routines of people living there, etc. Then, the burglar might purchase a weapon or lock-breaking tools and gather some like-minded people. But, when the burglar reaches the target house to break in, the police are there with handcuffs. *Behavior-based detection* works in the same way—trying to identify malware based on the *behavior* of a file. For instance, an mp3 file trying to modify a system file is unacceptable under normal circumstances; behavior-based detection would identify such behavior as malicious.

Behavior-based detection can also be divided into two further types with subtle differences.

Anomaly-based detection first determines what is considered *normal* behavior. Then, any deviation from the normal outline would be considered doubtful or anomalous. For example, if a program routinely does not create any additional files but one day surprisingly moves a file into one of the system folders, that action would be taken as an anomaly and the program would be marked as malware. Anomaly-based malware detection can be passive or active.

Specification-based detection mediates the behavior of programs, including system and application programs, according to a prefabricated policy. For example, the policy might disallow execution of files downloaded from a website specified by the person in charge of the computer system. Specification-based detection offers lots of flexibility but can only be handled by expert users.

Heuristic detection

Heuristic detection is used by some antivirus software to detect either already known malicious programs or new variants of existing malware families. This method detects malware by using certain heuristic techniques.

File emulation/sandbox testing allows a scanned file to run in a controlled fashion in an isolated virtual environment called a *sandbox*. While the file is running in the sandbox, its behavior can be judged without concern about harming the computer system, even if the file turns out to be malware. Sandboxing is also called *dynamic scanning* because it performs detection during runtime.

File analysis is a variant of sandboxing where, without sandboxing the file, specially designed software analyzes the file to determine its intent, destination, purpose, etc. This may require de-compilation of the file to examine its source code, to determine, for example, whether a file contains instructions in its code to delete some system files. The source code analyses of existing malware can also be compared with the source codes of files under scrutiny.

Generic signature detection identifies variants of known malware that have been tweaked slightly to disguise and bluff the malware signature database.

Whitelisting

Another emerging guard against malware threats is *whitelisting.* The above-mentioned methods focus on identifying malicious patterns and behavior in order to declare that a code is malware, meaning that every program or file is considered benign unless proven otherwise by its behavior or its content. Known malicious software is often *blacklisted*, meaning that the program, file, or application is not allowed to be downloaded, installed, or opened. Whitelisting is the opposite of blacklisting, reversing the approach.

Rather than looking for bad software in a world of good software, whitelisting prevents execution of all code except that which has been proven trustworthy. This approach circumvents the need to keep malware signatures up-to-date. Additionally, undesirable computer applications are barred, since they are not on the whitelist.

Since today's enterprise organizations rely on so many trusted applications, the challenges of implementing whitelisting rest with the system administrators' capability, likely with the aid of tools for automating the inventory and whitelist maintenance processes, to properly account for and maintain the list of trusted applications.

Pros and Cons of Antivirus Usage

Advantages

Securing a system with antivirus software provides some benefits for the upkeep of the system and comfort of usage. It is a safeguard against quite a few, if not all, security risks. Potential benefits include:

- *Real-time protection*: If there is no antivirus program on the system, files cannot be scanned as they are brought into the computer (i.e., *real-time*). Similarly, the programs are not scanned as they become active. Most antivirus software use a real-time scanner to shield the computer system against an infected file or program encountered in real time; it can be immediately deleted or moved into quarantine.

- *Boot-time scan*: Another feature of good antivirus software is a *boot-time scan* option. Today's viruses, in many cases, are so sophisticated and persistent that they duplicate themselves when they are deleted, as long as an operating system is functioning. However, with a boot-time scan, the antivirus software will stop the operating system and will restart the entire computer system. When the system restarts, the hard disks are scanned for viruses and other malware before the operating system starts running, allowing persistent malware to be deleted permanently.
- *Scanning of individual files*: With antivirus software, users can scan individual files or programs before interacting with them. This precaution can prevent the wide-scale spread of malware from infected executable files.
- *Safeguarding sensitive information*: Without an antivirus software on the system, users may run into malware that are intelligent enough to use machines in an organization to relay other forms of malware. Some malware have been known to try infecting everyone in an already-infected user's contact list. In some cases, most or all of the sensitive information may be uploaded to infected computers or botnets.

Challenges

While the importance of up-to-date antivirus software cannot be overemphasized, in today's environment, antivirus software also comes with a set of challenges, including:

- *False positives*: Occasionally, antivirus software will declare a legitimate program malware and prevent its normal functioning. This may cause serious trouble in a system where antivirus software has been configured to quarantine or remove malware by default. In such a case, there is a chance, though remote, that a system service could be incapacitated, potentially resulting in a slowed or malfunctioning complete system. Sometimes, important system functions, like software update installation, are disrupted by antivirus software. In that case, antivirus software might have to be disabled while such installation is underway. Normal functionality of some beneficial or benign software, such as firewalls and VPNs, may be hampered by active antivirus software.

- *Effectiveness*: No antivirus software can provide 100% protection against malware threats. Antivirus software cannot ever be thought of as foolproof protection. Antivirus software, even those using behavior-based detection and heuristic methods, lack guaranteed assurance against new malware. It is a common practice among malware authors to test the effectiveness of their products before release against top-of-the-line antivirus software.
- *Rootkits*: As mentioned in Chapter 5, detecting rootkits is a major challenge for antivirus software. Rootkits have privileged access to the computer and are not shown in the list of running applications. Even if detected, rootkits are difficult to remove from the system. They will always pose a challenge to antivirus software.
- *Damage to legitimate programs and data*: When antivirus software tries to repair an infected file, it sometimes damages the victim file while removing malware code. In such cases, damaged files can only be restored from existing backups, if available.
- *Firmware issues*: Active antivirus programs can interfere with the process of updating *firmware*—the computer system's permanent software programmed into a read-only format. Furthermore, any writeable firmware, like BIOS, can be infected by malicious code and require replacement of the BIOS chip.

Other Protection Mechanisms against Malware Attacks

The challenges posed by antivirus software usage should not, by any means, suggest that users should avoid using antivirus software. In today's environment, when most computer systems are connected to the Internet—the biggest gateway for malware—antivirus software is essential to a smooth, functioning system.

But antivirus software alone is not enough. The next few chapters will discuss ways to augment antivirus software to make defenses more formidable through other tools and mechanisms, such as firewalls, intrusion prevention/detection systems, and encryption.

CHAPTER

Cryptography

What is Cryptography?

Antivirus software is only the first necessary preventive step against today's malware threats. New malware is created every day, and most computer systems are online most, if not all, of the time. Other strategies are required in order to have anything close to a foolproof defense against cyberattacks.

This chapter briefly addresses the science and art of cryptography and how it relates to information security objectives. *Cryptography* is an ancient science and art of sending messages in a secret, enciphered, or disguised form understood only by the intended recipient, who can remove the disguise. Because cryptography is a vast field requiring serious and deliberate study, the discussion below only deals with the basics.

Understanding cryptography requires knowing the following terms:

Cryptanalysis

Closely related to cryptography is *cryptanalysis*—the study of breaking codes and ciphers used in encrypted messages. Cryptanalysis is a typical tool of malicious parties, making it imperative to study cryptanalysis in order to make stronger codes and excel in cryptography.

Cryptology

Cryptology encompasses both cryptography and cryptanalysis to study making codes and ciphers and the techniques used to break them. Figure 7.1 illustrates the relationships between cryptology, cryptography, and cryptanalysis.

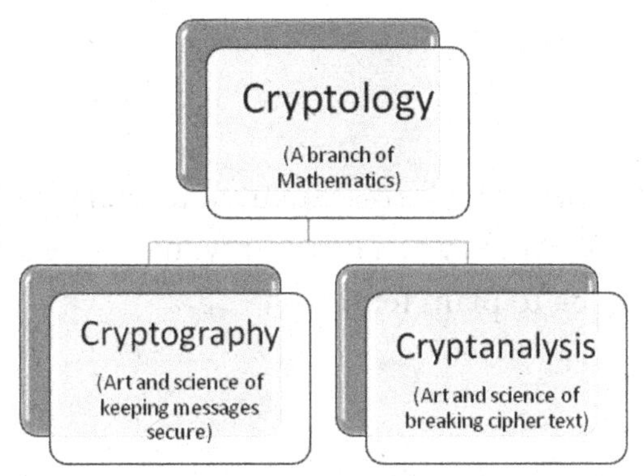

Figure 7.1: The relationships of cryptology, cryptography, and cryptanalysis

Plain text

Plain text is a piece of information in its original form, typically readable by anyone.

Cipher text

Cipher text is the coded (*encrypted*) message that travels from sender to receiver. It is supposedly not understandable by anyone who would intercept the message.

Encryption

Also called *enciphering*, this is the process of converting plain text into cipher. This process is done at the sender end before the message is sent to the receiver.

Decryption

Also called *deciphering*, this is the process of recovering plain text from cipher text.

Key

A *key* is a piece of private information used to encrypt plain text. The same key or the second key of a key pair would be needed to decrypt the cipher text back to plain text.

Key pairs

With *key pairs*, a sender first uses a private key to encrypt a message. The private key is the sender's own property, which no one else knows or can use. But the second key of the pair is a public key, accessible to trusted recipients and used only to decrypt the message. No one can decrypt the message encrypted by a person's private key except the one who has the associated public key, and vice versa.

Cryptographic algorithm

A *cryptographic algorithm* is a set of instructions and procedures used to encrypt a message. Plain text is fed to the cryptographic algorithm and encrypted through the sender's key. Cryptographic algorithms are public, in contrast with the individual keys used with an algorithm.

Types of Cryptographic Algorithms

Cryptographic algorithms can be categorized in different ways, primarily based on the number and types of keys. These classifications include:

- Secret Key (Symmetric) Cryptography (SKC)
- Public Key (Asymmetric) Cryptography (PKC)
- Hash Functions (One-Way Cryptography).

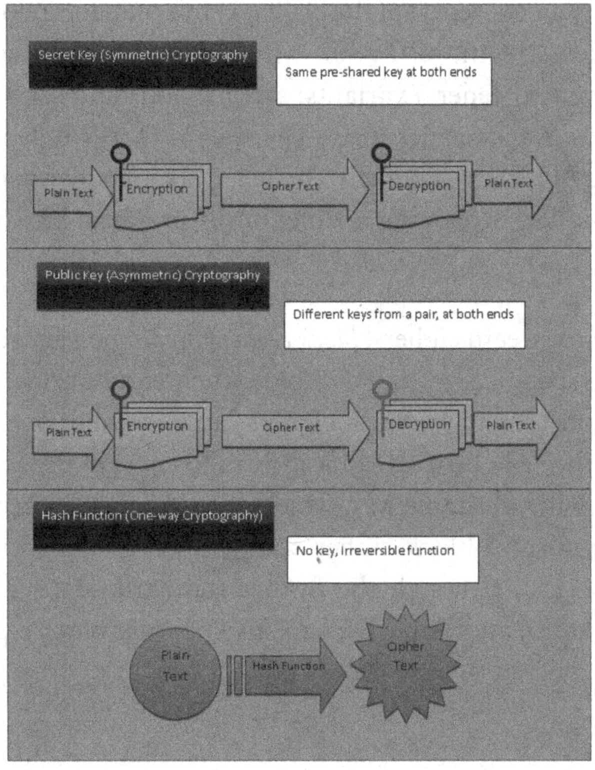

Figure 7.2: Types of cryptographic algorithms

Secret key cryptography (SKC)

In *secret key cryptography*, both encryption and decryption use the same key. First, the key must be shared through a secure channel. Next, the sender uses the key and the algorithm to encrypt the plain text before sending the cipher text to the recipient. The intended recipient then decrypts the cipher text to plain text using the shared key with the algorithm.

SKC can be further divided into *stream* and *block* ciphers. *Stream ciphers* continuously encrypt the plain text in a pseudorandom fashion with the key stream, bit by bit, while being transmitted. Stream ciphers have two general variants: synchronous and asynchronous. *Synchronous stream ciphers* use a key stream that is independent of the message bits; *asynchronous*, or *self-synchronous*, *stream ciphers* generate the key stream as a function of previous bits of the key stream.

In contrast to stream ciphers, *block ciphers* break messages down into blocks of a specific size (i.e., 128 bits), then encrypt one block at a time with the secret key. Block ciphers can be used in one of several modes, or they can be used in basic form to encrypt the same plain-text block with the same key, which should result in same cipher text.[14] The current block cipher standard is Advance Encryption Standard (AES), although the former standard, Data Encryption Standard (DES), and Triple DES are also popular block ciphers.[15]

---

[14] Examples of block cipher modes include Electronic Code Book (ECB), Cipher Block Chaining (CBC), Cipher Feedback (CFB), Output Feedback (OFB), and Counter Mode. A dedicated cryptography textbook would provide a more in-depth understanding of these different modes.

[15] A dedicated cryptography book would provide a more in-depth explanation about AES and DES.

Public key cryptography (PKC)

Considered a breakthrough in modern cryptology, *public key cryptography* (*PKC*) enables cryptographic communication over an insecure channel without requiring keys to be pre-shared, unlike SKC, which requires sharing a secret key through secure channels. In many practical scenarios, it is not possible, or, at the very least, it is extremely difficult, to securely issue shared keys to all intended communication parties. Keeping this problem in mind, cryptographer Whitfield Diffie and cryptologist Martin Hellman proposed a system that could enable sharing of secret keys over insecure channels, beginning the era of PKC. [16]

PKC relies on one-way functions, which are computationally infeasible to reverse. The functions are easier to implement but are mathematically beyond the computational power of today's machines to invert. Two computational problems normally used by PKC algorithms are multiplication factorization and exponentiation logarithms.

A simple example of PKC is when all users on a network have their own private and public keys:

> All the public keys are available at a server on the network, accessible to trusted users only. However, each user has a secret, private key only accessible to that user and not shared even with trusted users. To send a message, user X can encrypt using either his or her private key or recipient Y's public key. On the other end, Y has to decrypt the message using X's public key (if X has encrypted with his or her own private key) or Y's own private key (if X has encrypted with Y's public key). All trusted users can get the public keys of other trusted users from the secure vault on a network server designated for this purpose. In broadcast or multicast messages, the sender has to

[16] Diffie, Whitfield and Martin E. Hellman. "New directions in cryptography." Information Theory, IEEE Transactions on 22.6 (1976): 644-654.

> encrypt the message with his or her own private key so that all recipients may decrypt it using sender's public key. A message encrypted with the sender's own private key is assured to have origin authenticity, since no one else has access to a user's private key.

Another example of PKC's usefulness is a secure communication over the Internet:

> A user attempts to make a secure connection to a website's server. After receiving an approved public key by a public key issuing authority, the server sends its public key (known in this case as a *digital certificate*) to the user (neither the user nor a third party can calculate the private key). The user then uses the server's public key to propose, encrypt, and send a symmetric session key to the server. No one, not even the user who encrypted it, can decrypt this session key—except the server; the session key can only be decrypted with the server's secret, private key. Once the server receives and decrypts the symmetric session key sent by the user, the user and the server both have the session key, known only to each other. From here on, both will encrypt and decrypt using the session key, essentially using SKC.

Hash functions

Rather than using keys, *hash functions* calculate a fixed-length hash value against the plain text.[17] Hash functions are one-way, meaning it is computationally infeasible to invert the function and retrieve the plain text. Ideally, hash functions should have the following properties:

- Hash values should be easily computed using that function.
- It should be impossible to re-create the plain text from the hash.

---

[17] A *hash value* is a result of a calculation (*hash algorithm*) that can be performed on a string of text, electronic file, or entire hard drive contents.

- Any modification in the message should require recalculation of hash.
- Hash for each plain text should be unique.

Hash functions, due to their above-mentioned properties, are very effective at ensuring data integrity. Any change made to the contents of a message would make its hash different when calculated by the recipient. As it is highly unlikely that two different messages would yield the same hash, data integrity is ensured to the maximum. Certain hash functions are used in digital forensics and in some information or computer security utilities. Common hash functions today include Message Digest (MD) algorithms and Secure Hash Algorithms (SHA).[18]

Purpose of Cryptography

Cryptography is an important area of information security, addressing several of information security's basic goals. In fact, cryptography focuses on several of the information security foundations discussed in Chapter 1, including confidentiality, authentication, integrity, and accountability.

Confidentiality

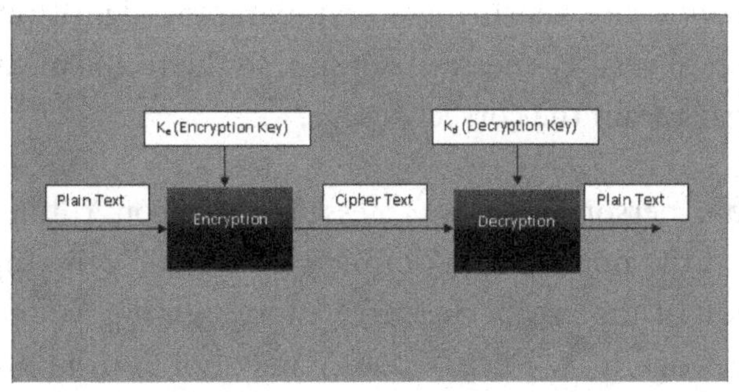

Figure 7.3: Confidentiality through cryptography

[18] A dedicated cryptography book would provide a more in-depth explanation of these and other hash functions.

Recalling the definition of confidentiality from Chapter 1, confidentiality is concerned with revealing information to users only according to their rights/roles. Information not intended for some particular user should be inaccessible to that user.

In cryptography, the sender or the information owner uses a cryptographic algorithm and a secret key to encrypt information before sending it to the recipient. Thus, anyone who is not the intended recipient cannot read the information, even if it is intercepted, because even if the type of cryptographic algorithm is known, the key is a secret known only to the intended parties. Since the intended recipient should have either the same key through which the message was encrypted or the second of a key pair (depending on the type of cryptographic algorithm used), the intended recipient will be able to decrypt the message to get the original plain text. In this way, a message can confidentially reach the intended recipients without access by others.

Authentication

Recall that authentication is another important computer security foundation, dealing with identifying users and assigning them access rights based on the nature of their roles, permissions, and tasks. Cryptography augments this idea through the use of *entry/ origin authentication*, ensuring a cryptographic algorithm includes information to verify a message's origin, so the recipient can be sure the message is from the correct source.

For example, person X sends a message to person Y, but person Z has adjusted the normal functioning of the system by stopping the transmission of the actual message, impersonating X, and sending Z's own message to Y. In this case, Y may not even know that the message received is from someone other than X. Notably, this is an attack against authentication, rather than against confidentiality, since Z has not necessarily read the content of the original message, only replaced the original message with a new one.

The problem could have been resolved through cryptography. If X had encrypted the message with a secret, private, key known to no one, but Y has the other, public, key paired with X's private key, then only Y could decrypt the message, using X's public key. That way, Y would be sure that the message originated with the correct source, X. Y could be sure of the source because no one else could have encrypted the message in such a way without X's private key.

Integrity

Cryptography focuses on authenticating not just data source or originator but also verifying a message's contents for correctness. This type of verification, also known as *content authentication*, augments the security foundation of integrity.

Cryptographic techniques can be conveniently employed to verify the integrity of information to ensure that data has not been altered during transmission or storage. For example, when a user is downloading information from the Internet, the user wants to download the complete package of information with no errors. Working to ensure an error-free download, the entity making this data available keeps a cryptographic hash value against the data and keeps it with the data. Since hash functions are one-way (irreversible) and are unique for each message, the cryptographic hash of the message allows the recipient, or downloader, in this case, to, if need be, calculate the hash of the downloaded data. If the hash of the received data calculated at the recipient's end is the same as that calculated at the sender's end (appended with the data), the integrity of the data is intact. If the hashes are different, then the recipient may ask for retransmission or discard the data altogether, depending on the situation.

Accountability

Remember that accountability means that no one in a system should be able to deny his actions or be falsely accused of something which they have not done.[19] In addition to ensuring confidentiality, authentication, and integrity, cryptographic means can also ensure system accountability:

> Supervisor X sends an email from his account to worker Y, asking him to go to a specific location on a particular day. However, when Y goes to that location, X admonishes Y for being absent from his office. Y mentions he received an order via email from X to go to that location; X denies sending any such email. However, the email can be seen in Y's inbox and X's outbox.

What could be the solution to avoid such a problem? Under normal circumstances, when the system is appropriately used and password-protected, *digital signatures* can be used to ensure that X cannot dispute sending these emails. Closely related to the ideas of origin authentication and private secret keys, a digital signature is accessible only to X. If X encrypts his message with his digital signature (usually in the form of a digital certificate), then the recipient can be sure about the origin of the message and, at the same time, X can be held accountable for sending the email, since no one else has access to his private signature.

[19] Refer to Chapter 1 for more about accountability and its role as part of the seven security foundations.

CHAPTER

8

Understanding Networks and Network Security

What is a Network?

Most of the previously discussed security dynamics apply primarily, if not exclusively, to individual computer systems. It is important to understand how those security dynamics become more complex and unpredictable when a computer system is connected to a network, especially a public network like the Internet.

Recall that *network security* uses physical and electronic preventive, protective, and curative measures to safeguard network infrastructure from unauthorized admission, exploitation, breakdown, failure, or disclosure.[20] Network security is complex, requiring a basic understanding of computer network planning, designing, deployment, operation, and maintenance.

A *computer network* is formed when two or more computers connect with each other to share resources (such as a printer or hard drive), information (such as documents or media files), or services (such as some application software). The computers may be connected through cables, or they may be wirelessly connected.

[20] Refer to Chapter 1 for a definition and brief overview of network security.

Network types based on topology

Computer networks can be categorized based on their layout, or *topology.* Network topologies are star, ring, mesh, and bus. In *star* topology, each computer is connected to a central *node.* A node can be a computer system or some other device, such as a printer. Every node has a unique network identifier, sometimes called a *Data Link Control* (*DLC*) *address* or *Media Access Control* (*MAC*) *address.*

Ring is a network topology in which every computer is connected to two other computers, one on either side, thereby forming a ring of computers. *Bus* topology is an open ring, meaning computers are connected in a line. Finally, in *mesh* topology, computers are connected to every other computer in a network. Differences in topology affect network failures, speed, and administration.

Network types based on size and scope

Another way of classifying computer networks is to differentiate them on the basis of their size and scope of operation. *Local area networks* (*LAN*), also known as *wired networks*, use Ethernet cables and one or more network switches to connect computers located within the same premises, such as within a school building. On the other hand, *wide area networks* (*WAN*), also known as *wireless networks*, use a variety of different connectivity methods and employ network switches and routers or gateways to spread over a bigger area with a higher number of computers, such as all of computers of a bank spread over many branches in various cities. Finally, the largest network with the widest scope is the *Internet*—a global network of networks.

The OSI model

The *Open Systems Interconnection* (*OSI*) *model* is a framework that acts as a reference model for applications to communicate with each other over a network. The OSI model divides the process of communication between two end points into seven layers of functionality. This means that a message generated from a host application on a source machine would traverse from the top layer to the bottom layer of that machine; be routed through the network; and, after reaching the destination machine, traverse the layers from bottom to the application at the top. This process is illustrated in Figure 8.1.

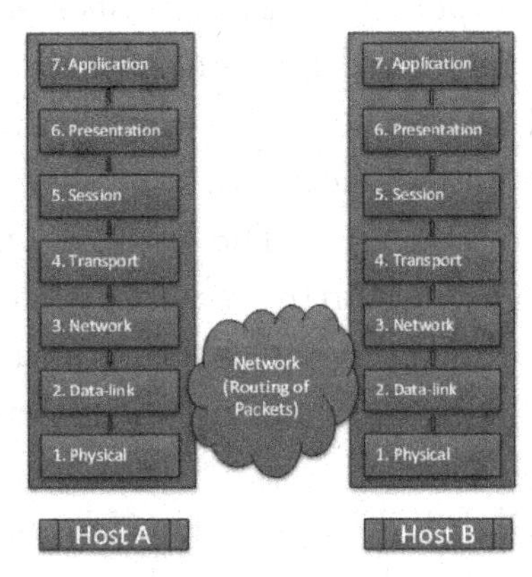

Figure 8.1: Host A's application transmitting to host B's application

The functionality of the layers is provided by various protocols at each layer. The role of each layer of the OSI model is briefly explained below:

- *Layer 7—Application layer*: At the *application layer*, the communication partners are earmarked or identified, and capacity of the network is judged. This layer should not be confused with the actual application trying to communicate; rather, it is a set of services that an application uses. However, some applications may also perform application-layer functionality.
- *Layer 6—Presentation layer*: The *presentation layer* is mostly part of operating system, working to convert inward and outward *datagrams* from one presentation format to another.[21]

[21] A datagram is a basic transfer unit associated with a packet-switched network. The delivery, arrival time, and order of arrival need not be guaranteed by the network.

- *Layer 5—Session layer*: The *session layer* establishes, synchronizes, and ends conversations or sessions. Authentication and reconnection after interruption are also functions of this layer. Over the Internet, *Transmission Control Protocol* (*TCP*) and *User Datagram Protocol* (*UDP*) provide such services for most applications.
- *Layer 4—Transport layer*: The *transport layer* packages data into packets and then delivers the packets, including checking for errors. TCP and UDP also provide these services on the Internet for most applications.
- *Layer 3—Network layer*: The *network layer* addresses and steers data, sending it on the correct path towards its intended destination and receiving inward transmissions at packet level. The *IP layer* is the name of the network layer on the Internet.
- *Layer 2—Data-link layer*: The *data-link layer* builds connections through the physical network, stuffing packets into digital data transmission units called *network frames.* This layer can be divided into two sub-layers based on functionality: the *Logical Link Control* (*LLC*) *layer* and the *Media Access Control* (*MAC*) *layer.* Ethernet operates at layer 2.
- *Layer 1—Physical layer*: The *physical layer* refers to the actual hardware transmitting and receiving the bit stream over the network in electrical, optical, or radio form.

Important Devices Related to Computer Networks

Establishing and maintaining a network requires various software and hardware devices. Different devices are necessary depending on the size and scope of the network, including the number of users, the amount and speed of traffic on the network, and nature of services and resources offered by the network.

Ethernet card

An *Ethernet card* is installed in an individual computer system to enable it to connect to the network. The card typically includes a port for connecting an Ethernet cable to access wired LAN and/or a small antenna for transmission and reception to access wireless LAN. Ethernet cards are also called *network identification cards* (*NIC*). All NICs come with a MAC address used to identify the hosts on the network.

Repeater

Repeaters are employed between two network segments for signal regeneration. They work only at the physical layer of the OSI model.[22]

Hub

A *hub* is used in small wired networks to forward all network traffic received to all other computers or devices on the network. It has no intelligence for making decisions. All of the computers on the network are connected to the hub.

Switch

A *switch* is a network device that gives connections to multiple computers to form a network. It works at layer 2 of OSI model, i.e., the data link layer, meaning it can only handle a single LAN.[23] A switch's capacity of connections ranges from eight to sixty, depending on the cost and type of device. Switches may appear identical to hubs but, unlike hubs, switches have intelligence and do not just forward all network traffic. Instead, switches examine the traffic and send it

---

[22] Refer to Figure 8.1.

[23] Refer to Figure 8.1.

only the destination computer, thereby reducing traffic considerably. Switches normally use MAC addresses and work with the router to maintain a table for matching IP addresses to MAC addresses.

Router/Gateway

Routers, or *gateways*, are employed to make communication possible between networks in spite of differences in topology, size, protocols, or physical characteristics. Routers make sure that traffic of data packets is sent throughout the appropriate *transmission path*, consisting of different networks and devices, to reach the intended destination.

At the network layer, the packets travel from network to network according to their destination IP addresses. Routers, for the purpose of directing the packets, examine the destination IP address of incoming packets and forward them to paths as stored in their *routing tables*, maintained by each router by learning from the network traffic.

Wireless access points

Wireless access points (APs) are similar to network switches and routers, but wireless APs enable network communication only for wireless clients on a network, as opposed to on a LAN. Wireless APs use antennas to send and receive messages through radio signals.

Firewall

A *firewall* is a hardware device or a software application meant to prevent intrusion of malicious parties or malware in the garb of ordinary network traffic.[24]

---

[24] Firewalls are examined and discussed in much greater depth in Chapter 9.

Network Threats

Networks provide a computer system and its users access to many functions and automation capabilities. However, with increased access and automation come the danger of increased threats and vulnerabilities. To take measures against network threats and plug the vulnerabilities, users must understand them. Some of the prevailing network threats are described below.

Changed security dynamics

A computer system that is not connected to the network is like a walled-off city; there are few entry points, it is well-guarded, and it is under observation. Users can easily protect an isolated computer system because its threat environment is visible and obvious.

By contrast, a computer system connected to a network is like a city with no perimeter; there are many entry points, and people and goods frequently come in and go out. Therefore, checking and monitoring mechanisms need to be more elaborate and comprehensive, catering to all possible situations.

Denial of service (DoS) attacks

Denial of service (*DoS*) attacks are perhaps the most common network attacks. DoS targets a system's availability, denying a system's services to its trusted and legitimate users.[25]

Sometimes services become unavailable due to hardware failure, power failure, or some other circumstances under the system staff's control. Other times, there is a break in services due to faulty coding, developer bugs in the software, or incorrect system configuration.

[25] Refer to Chapter 1 for more about availability and its role as part of the seven security foundations.

Despite service becoming unavailable, these types of problems are not DoS attacks. DoS attacks are when unavailability occurs due to enemy action or malicious activity.

An attacker's goal with a DoS attack is to either disrupt or degrade the service. Attackers typically seek to cause as much harm as possible by aiming at the most critical services offered by a targeted network.

Normally, a DoS attack takes place by overwhelming the target server with false (or possibly technically correct) requests for services. A DoS attack is successful only if the attacker generates more requests than the server's capacity can handle. Otherwise, the server will continue providing services to its legitimate users, possibly with a slight deterioration. This is why attackers often rely on zombie computers linked into a botnet to execute a Distributed Denial of Service (DDoS) attack by making all of the computers in the botnet simultaneously request the target's services.[26] Other popular DoS attack methods include:

- *Direct/Indirect*: In the simplest form of DoS attack, an attacker tries to flood the victim with unsolicited traffic from the attacker's own IP address (*direct DoS attack*) or through a spoofed (fake or hoax) IP address (*indirect DoS attack*).
- *Intermediary*: In this case, the attacker uses *intermediaries*, such as zombie computers and botnets, to attack the victim. Sometimes, when the number of zombie computers is too high, an additional layer of compromised hosts, known as *handler* or *command and control servers*, is used to control the botnet.
- *Attack through malformed packets*: In this method, the attacker sends malformed packets of information to the victim computer system, causing it to crash. For example, ping of death was once a popular attack that used an illegally

[26] Refer to the discussion of zombie computers and botnets in Chapter 5.

long IP packet to cause an operating system to crash, thereby causing denial of service to users.[27]

- *Reflected:* This attack uses legitimate services to flood the victim with requests. For example, the attacker sends requests to email, DNS, or web servers from the spoofed address of a victim system. Now, all the replies will go from the servers to the victim system. Figure 8.2 illustrates a reflected DoS attack.

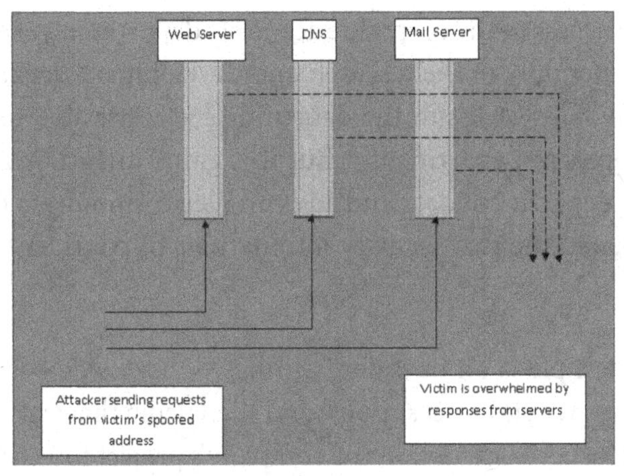

Figure 8.2: Reflected DoS attack

Unauthorized access

Unauthorized access is the act of gaining entry to a system or a network without permission, including using illegal or unapproved means, whether by an attacker outside the network (not part of the organization) or by an authorized user, to gain more privileges. In a networked system with plenty of resources, services, and users,

[27] For more information about ping of death, *see* Lippmann, Richard P., et al. "Evaluating intrusion detection systems: The 1998 DARPA off-line intrusion detection evaluation." DARPA Information Survivability Conference and Exposition, 2000. DISCEX'00. Proceedings. Vol. 2. IEEE, 2000.

unauthorized access can lead to disastrous results, wreaking havoc with resources and services.

Unauthorized access violates the security foundation of confidentiality and might also lead to breaches of integrity and availability. Therefore, it is vital for a system administrator to address all security loopholes leading to unauthorized access.

An example of unauthorized access by an internal host can be person X trying to access to the corporate accounts department, even though X is a member only of the research and development department. X should only have access to the data and services related to research and development department.[28] But if X gains unauthorized access to account department data and adds an illegal amount to his salary, he has violated the two security foundations of confidentiality and integrity.

Another example is an outsider gaining X's access by breaking the password of a wireless access point and then using that access to enter the corporate network, obtain the company's project forecast, and sell it to its competitors. This case is a violation of confidentiality.

Man-in-the-middle (MITM) attack

In a *man-in-the-middle* (*MITM*) attack, an attacker intercepts the network communication between two hosts and takes control to relay messages between the hosts while leaving them unaware of the attacker's presence. This can help the attacker access and perhaps modify critical information. MITM is also called *session hijacking*. E-commerce and banking sites are frequently targeted by MITM

[28] Refer to Chapter 3 for discussions on role-based access control and the principle of least permissions.

attacks, often trying to capture login credentials or credit card data. Some of the most popular MITM attack methods include:

- *Malware*: By distributing malware that gives an attacker access to users' web browsers, an attacker can access the data being sent and received.
- *Exploiting weak authentication of a network device*: An attacker can easily break through the authentication of wireless routers or other access points (APs) if the AP is using obsolete network security protocols. Control of a network device such as an AP gives an attacker enough access to eavesdrop and even modify the network communication.
- *Evil twin attack*: In public places like airports and restaurants, free Internet access is normally provided through open access wireless APs. One MITM attack method is launched by setting up a twin wireless AP with the same ID. A few clients will connect to this evil twin instead of the legitimate AP, allowing the attacker to act as the man in the middle, able to view and potentially modify all network traffic.
- *Rogue IPv6 router*: Most computer systems are set up by default to prefer connecting to an available IPv6 router rather than an IPv4 router. Thus, in a network that only includes IPv4 routers, an attacker can use the same information to insert a rogue IPv6 router into a network, automatically rerouting most, if not all, network traffic through the rogue router. This would not only enable the attacker to launch a MITM attack; the attacker could also send users to selected phishing sites.

Business Benefits of Network Security

Corporate environments flourish when they employ a networked, automated solution designed to take advantage of the benefits of a computer network while also addressing the potential threats and vulnerabilities involved in network communications. The need for network security cannot be denied. With secure networks, a corporation's data will be protected, and clients' personal data will be safe from unauthorized access. Advantages of secure networks include:

- Protecting personal information and client credentials, such as credit card data, from unauthorized access increases client confidence.
- Sharing information and services in a reliable way that even remote employees can access allows a corporation's productivity to significantly increase.
- Networks protected against DoS attacks are, therefore, always available to their clients; they are considered reliable and dependable, increasing client confidence.
- Security techniques, including a robust information security policy, can essentially protect against confidentiality breaches, leaked trade secrets, and even rogue employee threats.
- A hardened and tested network can result in sped-up business processes, reduction in employee stress, and increased productivity, due to fewer concerns about the nuisance of daily security breaches; the cost of hardening the network can be paid back in the advantages within a matter of months.
- It is easier and simpler to extend and enhance the area of influence of a network that is well-planned, security-hardened, and well-distributed into segments and areas to facilitate future scalability.

Firewalls

What is a Firewall?

The literal meaning of *firewall* is a partition designed to prevent the spread of fire. In IT and information/computer security terms, a firewall is hardware or software designed to protect systems from unwanted transmission of data packets based on criteria derived from policy guidelines. Firewalls need to perform in real time, which means that they require reasonable computational power and sufficient memory space. Therefore, to perform its function properly, the firewall will ideally be an independent piece of hardware with its own dedicated resources, rather than a software application sharing the computer system's resources. Today's hardware firewalls are often included as part of routers, providing the firewalls with access to high computational power, enormous memory, and their own operating systems.

How are Firewalls Used?

Today's networks are like cities with a number of entry points where people and goods keep coming in and going out.[29] A firewall is a

[29] Refer to Chapter 8 for an examination and discussion of networks and network security.

network device that acts like a guard on some, if not all, entry points. The amount invested in a guard typically depends on the level of threat, the surrounding environment, and the value of assets in need of protection. The same analogy can be drawn with the quality of the firewall. If the threat is from a public network, especially the Internet, and the assets are a corporation's resources, then users should be prepared to invest in top-of-the-line firewalls.

However, even the best firewalls can be rendered useless if they are employed with carelessness and lack of expertise. Correct configuration is what makes a firewall a formidable guard against threats. Configuration not only requires excellent technical skills but also an understanding of any relevant security policies. To master the configuration skills of a particular firewall or firewalls in general, users must first understand the basic principles of firewall filtering and other functions.

Basic operation of a firewall

As illustrated in Figure 9.1, a firewall's strategy is to examine data packets and make a pass-or-deny decision based on certain criteria. The packets that are considered clean and safe are allowed to pass, whereas the packets that are considered to be harmful and malicious are simply dropped. Firewalls maintain a log of dropped packets by default. Administrators should study the log regularly, examine the dropped packets, learn why the packets have been dropped, and, if quite a few malicious packets are from the same source, discover and potentially block the address of that particular source.

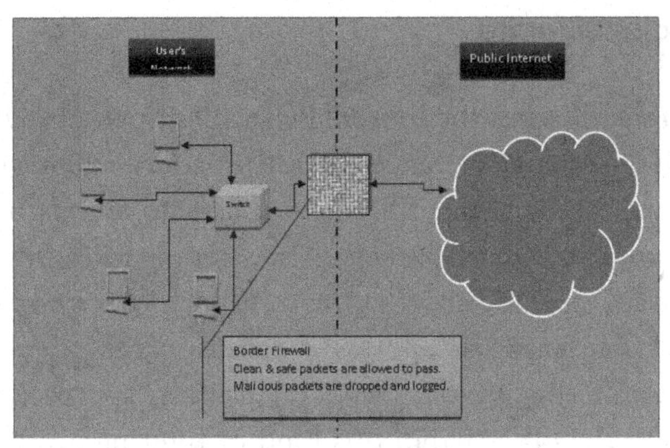

Figure 9.1. Basic firewall operation

Ingress and egress filtering

Firewalls have two sides: the outer side and the inner side. Incoming packets are normally examined from the outer side to determine whether they are safe. Such filtering is called a firewall's *ingress filtering* mechanism. However, a border firewall should work both ways, like a good guard on the border of a country, and check the network's outgoing data packets too. Such filtering by the firewall is called *egress filtering.*

Why is egress filtering needed? Going back to the example of a border guard, in addition to ensuring that people and goods don't illegally enter the country, the guard should also be checking that no goods are illegally exported. Similarly, a firewall should also be configured to detect any malicious packets or critical information sent by a computer system or network. The need for egress filtering cannot be denied.

Common Firewall Techniques

Filtering is the most basic function of a firewall. However, today's firewalls typically use more than one filtering mechanism. These mechanisms are described below.

Static packet filtering

In *static packet filtering*, the firewall looks at one packet at a time and examines it out of context. Since the traffic pattern will not be known to the firewall, static packet filtering is unable to ascertain an attack pattern from a stream of packets. Also, static packet filtering only examines a few specific areas in the transport layer and in internet layer headers (such as the IP address).[30] Because of these disadvantages, static packet filtering is typically not the primary approach of today's firewalls. On the other hand, this kind of filtering is still effective against certain specific attacks, like *echo messages* (*ICMP*) from attackers outside the network.[31] Since static packet filtering does still have these uses, it is currently used as a secondary filtering mechanism augmenting the firewall's primary filtering mechanism or to support the load of a firewall at the border of huge network.

Stateful packet filtering

Stateful packet filtering concentrates on the stream of data packets, rather than isolated packets. It examines the packets intelligently, considering their context, i.e., whether a packet is a part of a *handshake* (an exchange of a specific type of packets) between two hosts, part of an already established communication between two hosts, or a part of a connection-terminating sequence.

For example, technically speaking, normal TCP communication between two hosts takes place only after a *handshake*.[32] Because stateful packet filtering examines packets with reference to context, a firewall can detect a malicious communication attempt based on

---

[30] Refer to Chapter 8 for a more in-depth explanation of the transport layer of the OSI model.

[31] ICMP attacks are commands sent by an attacker to discover whether there is a host at a particular IP address.

[32] Refer to Chapter 8 for a discussion of TCP communication as part of the session layer of the OSI model.

an incomplete or improper handshake. Since stateful packet filtering focuses on connection, the firewall investigates at the transport layer (layer 4) where the connections between hosts are established, rather than at the network layer (layer 3) of the OSI stack.[33] Such connections are made through host computers' *sockets*—an IP address plus the port number at which the application is sending and receiving packets.

By default, a stateful packet filtering mechanism would disallow all connection attempts from external addresses to internal destinations, but it would allow connection attempts from internal hosts to external destinations. Additional filtering rules, called *access control lists* (*ACLs*), can be added by network administrators to supersede the defaults, depending on relevant needs, such as if a corporation wants to allow an external client to make connections with the internal hosts, or if the corporation would like to block connection attempts to phishing sites from internal hosts.

The low cost and high safety standards of stateful packet filtering make it an integral part of today's firewalls.

Network address translation (NAT)

Network address translation (*NAT*) is not a filtering technique, but it offers a great deal of protection against network attacks. A NAT firewall keeps internal IP addresses and port numbers confidential from the external world by altering the *source socket address* (IP address plus port number) of all outgoing traffic. This change in source socket address is based on a table maintained by the firewall, called a *translation table*, that also allows external responses to be marked back to the correct host.

[33] Refer to Figure 8.1.

NAT is not a filtering mechanism, but it does provide security-related benefits. For example, some attackers use packet sniffers immediately outside the network's entry and exit points to gain the IP addresses and port numbers of the network's hosts and learn the complete layout of the network for future attack options. But, with a NAT firewall, such an opportunity would be denied to the attacker; network addresses and port numbers are different outside the network.

Also, unlike some other firewall filters, NAT is totally transparent to outside and inside hosts, meaning it does not usually interfere with routine work. But certain protocols, like IPSec, VoIP, etc., can be hampered by NAT if necessary configuration settings are not adopted.[34]

Application proxy firewalls

The firewall techniques discussed so far are limited to OSI layer 3 (network layer) and layer 4 (transport layer).[35] However, network attacks can also occur at layer 7, the application layer, through a web application accessed by a client. *Application proxy firewalls* act like a middleman for client/server communication, where clients are internal hosts and servers are external. Application proxy firewalls act like a server for the internal client and like a client for the external server. They examine all of the transmitted content and make stop-or-pass decisions. The content can be inspected based on comparing URLs against blacklisted URLs and scripts for any malicious intent.

However, application proxy firewalls are limited by slow operation (due to the number of client/server communications taking place), and they affect only a few applications, such as those based in protocols like http or smtp. A better use of an application proxy firewall is to employ it with an internal server to examine all incoming traffic to

[34] Some of these protocols are explored in greater depth in Chapter 11.

[35] Refer to Figure 8.1.

that server from the outside. Incoming traffic from clients can be examined for malicious scripts, SQL injection attacks, and uploading of files through *POST commands* (used in HTTP protocol to send data to a server).

Today's stateful packet filtering firewalls often also include limited application proxy filtering.

Circuit-level gateways

Circuit-level gateways work at OSI level-5, the session layer.[36] These firewalls are like socket filters that monitor handshake mechanisms to confirm whether a session is legitimate. They operate similarly to stateful packet inspection.

Advantages and Limitations of Firewalls

Advantages

A network employing firewalls will definitely have security advantages, including:

- A first line of defense against external threats
- Fewer areas to concentrate security and incident response, since entry and exit points are controlled by the firewall
- A cost-effective way to ensure resource and data security and to augment other security features, like antivirus programs, host-hardening actions, and encryption of data, to create a formidable defense against external threats
- Additional security benefits from high-end firewalls, including antivirus protection, intrusion detection/prevention, etc.

---

[36] Refer to Figure 8.1.

Limitations

Firewalls also suffer from limitations, including:

- Firewalls should not be taken as a total security solution. They cannot protect against every threat and should not be used to create a false sense of security.
- Firewalls may not protect against general insider attacks; they are created to focus on securing network perimeters.
- Firewalls do not typically protect against malware, and, in fact, they may also be affected by a malware attack.
- Firewalls may become a nuisance by not allowing legitimate applications to function properly, tempting users to disable the firewall.
- Firewall filters are designed to protect against straightforward attacks. They cannot detect backdoors within network devices.
- Internet access through personal connections like GPRS[37], wireless access points, etc. is not guarded by firewalls; firewalls are employed nearly exclusively at the perimeters of wired networks.

[37] GPRS or *General Packet Radio Service* is a popular packet-oriented mobile data service.

CHAPTER

Intrusion Detection and Prevention Systems

What are Intrusion Detection and Prevention Systems?

Firewalls are a good at protecting networked computer systems against threats. But they are only the first step of better security architecture, not the end. Network administrators should consider the types of security attacks firewalls face, both daily and over a period of time.

A firewall's strength and ability to thwart attacks depend on the sophistication of its filtering mechanism and its processing power. Early firewalls were merely static packet filters with limited processing power; then came the era of stateful packet inspection techniques implemented over high-end machines. But as firewall filtering techniques have improved, so too have attack methods. A new type of filtering mechanism was needed to replace stateful packet filtering: an *intrusion prevention system* (IPS).

IPS is more comprehensive and reliable than the earlier generations of firewalls by virtue of superior pass or deny decision strategy. IPS can prevent attacks which could bypass earlier stateful packet inspection methods. IPSs developed from the earlier intrusion detection system (IDS) used in homes and offices to detect suspicious movements that could indicate burglaries.

This chapter introduces IPS and IDS, covering their basic operation and various types and categories, while also addressing what makes intrusion detection/prevention systems a better, more sophisticated choice than a normal firewall.

Intrusion Detection System (IDS)

If a firewall is a guard standing at an entry/exit point, stopping people from entering the building based on credible evidence as per the criteria given to him by management, an IDS would be a police officer who not only catches criminals but also keeps an eye on suspicious activity and keeps superiors duly informed about such activity.

Translating this analogy into technical language, firewalls inspect packets and prevent them from entering based on provided criteria, either factory default or added by the administrator. On the other hand, an IDS tends to identify packets that are not actually attack packets but are suspicious. An IDS may further investigate the suspicious packets, as would a good police detective.

How does an IDS work?

An IDS is a proactive defense mechanism that inspects network traffic and logs to detect suspicious activity and warn the administrators of the detected threats. The IDS does not only examine alarming suspicious activity on the network; some hosts have an IDS too, protecting the computer system against unwanted and illegitimate access by informing the administrator of doubtful and untrustworthy usage.

However, the IDS is not an active tool, only a passive monitor. An IDS is only an early-warning system, designed to detect suspicious activity over and above firewalls' ability to stop malicious packets. An IDS is like a security camera capturing all of the activity in a parking lot. To take action against unwanted activity, someone has to observe the camera feed and see those activities taking place.

IDS functions

An IDS performs four major functions. These functions may be performed by a single device, or, for efficiency, they may be divided among different pieces of hardware.

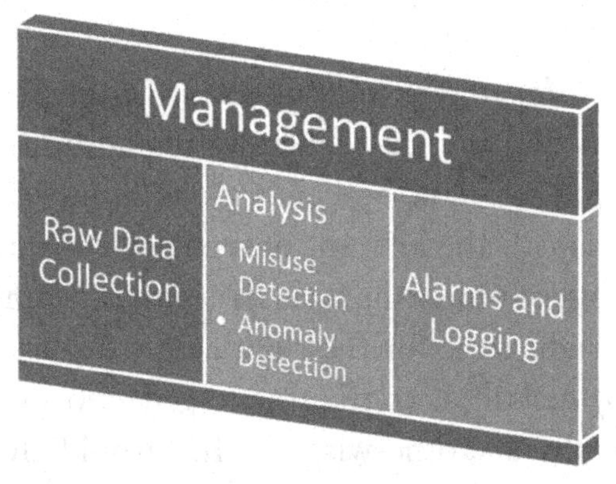

Figure 10.1. IDS functions

- *Data Collection*: The IDS records information about specific events and activities, such as encounters with a suspicious packet or an attempt to log on to some internal resource. This record is sequential and contains data in raw form, which can be examined by the administrator to learn about all of the activities and review incident responses.
- *Analysis*: IDS-collected data is analyzed by the IDS automatically and, based on the analysis, it issues warnings. An IDS uses two main types of analysis algorithms: misuse detection and anomaly detection:

- *Misuse detection*, also called *attack signature method*, compares the computer system or network's traffic pattern against the IDS's attack signature database. The IDS is supposed to have a database record of possible attack patterns signatures. Buffers are employed to keep copies of traffic patterns. If the traffic pattern matches a record in the database, a warning is issued.
- *Anomaly detection* has a record of benign traffic patterns and reports any deviation from the benign traffic patterns as an anomaly and, therefore, suspicious. However, with so much network traffic and such a variety of attack patterns, anomaly detection is considered less effective than misuse detection.

- *Output/Alarm*: The output phase of the IDS is linked to the remedial measure taken by the administrator. A huge collection of data and enormous computational power, coupled with the amount of memory consumed, would be meaningless unless the IDS warned the system administrator at the right time for the right cause. The catch is that the IDS, by default, is configured to generate an alarm only for serious threats; otherwise, the IDS would always alarm the administrator.

Not all IDS alarms mean something is wrong. An IDS indicates suspicious activities based on heuristics and leaves the administrator to decide whether the suspicion is a legitimate threat. The IDS should prepare plenty of information for the administrator to be able to make a decision.

Apart from warning through alarms, an IDS should log all subtle warnings that do not generate alarms. The administrator reads the logs to understand the nature of those threats as well. This way, the administrator gains threat analysis experience and receives insight for optimum IDS configuration.

- *Management*: An IDS must be continually managed by administrative staff. Based on the logs generated as part of the output/alarm function, the IDS must be regularly configured and fine-tuned for better performance. An IDS may be a nuisance to the administrator, but it can really prove its worth only if there is human interaction on regular basis.

Distributed IDS

A simple IDS, usually for just a single computer system, confines all four IDS functions into one piece of equipment. But, in the case of a network with multiple hosts, a *distributed IDS* keeps sensors at multiple devices and acts as a central monitor for the entire network.

All of the devices to be monitored by the distributed IDS house a *software agent*. These agents collect, store, and pass on data to the central manager. At times, these agents also carry out individual analysis and reporting/alarm-generation tasks.

A *manager* is placed at a central location to collect and log data. Because agents send data to the manager in the form of logs, the manager's log file is called the *integrated log file*. The manager's role is pivotal in the distributed IDS—performing a consolidated analysis of all of the logs. Then, based on the consolidated analysis, the manager generates reports and alarms if needed. Moreover, the manager is responsible for all of the distributed IDS's configuration settings and fine-tuning, including the software agents of individual machines.

Agents and the manager communicate in either *batch type* or *real time*. In batch-type communication, the agents keep the log files with them for some time, perhaps a few hours or more, and pass them on to the manager at a specified time, creating less traffic on the network. On the other hand, in real-time communication between agents and manager, the agents pass on the incident reports as soon as the events occur, resulting in more network traffic but also added security for the system.

Network IDS

Network intrusion detection systems examine and report packets of data when they traverse the network. Unlike a distributed IDS that installs agents on each network device, a network IDS installs agents at various network entry and exit points.

For example, one type of network IDS could install agents at all of the network switches and routers and install a few more agents at the network's cardinal paths. The good news is that the network IDS would have maximum coverage in terms of network traffic monitoring, since all possible entry and exit points, coupled with network junctions, would be handled. However, it would be too expensive and require too much effort to install agents at all switches and routers in a network used by a large organization, which means there would likely be too many dead areas left in the network—areas not under direct observation.

Host IDS

Since network IDS is unable to fully address all threats, one way to augment the system is, instead of protecting the routes, to protect the critical resource itself; in other words, use a *host intrusion detection system*. Host IDSs are used on critical hosts, such as servers. A host IDS protects the critical resource, provides maximum possible threat detection for a single host, and assists in adding safeguards and remedial measures. However, because the main focus of host IDS is a particular host, it cannot give a complete picture of a network for threats and, since it is nowhere near as extensive as network IDS, host IDS can also be compromised more easily.

IDS management

While purchasing and installing IDS can seem easy, managing an IDS for optimal performance can be quite cumbersome and demanding.

- *Configuring for precision*: It is difficult to configure an IDS to provide maximum protection with minimum false warning. IDS *precision* makes the IDS trustworthy and reliable. An IDS is most often removed from a system when it gives false positive warnings more often than it detects actual threats. The reverse of precision is configuring the IDS to detect more false negatives, considering real threats to be too subtle to report. In a nutshell, precision configuration is the best way to get the maximum value out of an IDS.
- *Remove irrelevant rules*: The default configuration of an IDS reports each and every threat. However, if a network does not face some specific type of threat, the irrelevant rules should be removed from the IDS. For example, a computer system or network not hosting websites can remove the rule to detect threats on port 80 (http traffic).
- *Attack signatures*: Networks using an IDS should keep the attack-signature database updated so that the IDS can detect new attack patterns.
- *Adequate processing power*: As the number of attacks grow, an IDS's performance might deteriorate due to limited computing power. As mentioned earlier, an IDS is typically a high-end machine with sufficient memory space. If the IDS is unable to perform when it is most needed, it creates a dangerous false sense of security.
- *Log files*: Other than computing power and memory space, the IDS badly needs large amounts of storage space. Because the IDS continuously records log files and performs raw data collection, it will typically fill up any allocated storage very quickly. While an IDS normally uses compression to handle space constraints, it becomes difficult and time-consuming

for the IDS to keep track of older attack patterns and suspicious activities.

IDS limitations

- *False positives*: An IDS generating a large amount of warnings and alarms can quickly become a nuisance for the administrator. Since many warnings may be irrelevant to the administrator, the administrator might stop paying attention to the IDS alarms, assuming they are most likely false positives. Therefore, an IDS is best configured based on the peculiarities of that specific system or network—requiring a combination of effort, expertise, and IDS experience.
- *Heavy processing*: Even though an IDS is a passive inspection machine, it requires heuristics to identify suspicious activity. Suspicious patterns can only be identified by inspecting a large amount of traffic, meaning the IDS requires high computing power and significant memory. These costs are important factors when deciding to employ an IDS in addition to firewalls.

Intrusion Prevention Systems

IDS vs. IPS

While an IDS only detects threats and attacks, an intrusion prevention system (IPS) both detects and prevents attacks. One analogy comparing IDS and IPS looks at different kinds of dogs. A dog that observes a theft or some suspicious activity and barks an alarm is like an IDS. The owner (or IDS administrator) may not pay any attention to the alarm and, thus, might have to pay the consequences if the attack is successful. On the other hand, a dog that not only barks at the thieves but also attacks them is like an IPS. The dog's owner (or IPS administrator) is also more likely to be notified and pay attention to the incident.

IPS functions

IDSs and IPSs both rely on the same basic principle—an attack or threat must first be detected before it can be prevented. Therefore, an IPS uses similar techniques as an IDS to detect an attack, but then it aggressively defends against the attack to prevent damage.

Another difference between IDSs and IPSs is the way they are deployed in a computer system. An IDS may be employed to monitor traffic or a particular host, but it is not required to be on the actual traffic path, as it never stops the traffic. However, since an IPS also needs to prevent the attack, it is deployed right in the traffic path to prevent traffic from progressing, if needed.

IPS processing power

As mentioned in the previous section, an IDS requires high computing power. An IPS is even more processor-intensive than an IDS. An IPS normally uses *application-specific integrated circuits* (*ASICs*) to implementing hardware filtering, allowing the IPS to remain effective and inline, even in a high volume of traffic.

The problem with false positives

While an IDS might have a problem with false positives, IPS false positives create an even bigger nuisance. While an IDS only generates false alarms as a result of false positive, an IPS will prevent the traffic altogether.

To avoid this problem, administrators must use the correct configuration settings. For example, IDSs and IPSs can detect a few types of attacks, such as denial of service (DoS) attacks, with sufficient confidence and without any problems.[38] Therefore, the IPS can be configured to block only these specific types of attacks

[38] Refer to Chapter 8 for a discussion about DoS attacks in greater depth.

and deal with any other attacks or threats like an IDS (sending a warning).

How an IPS prevents intrusions

An IPS can prevent intrusions through multiple methods. In most cases, when the IPS detects the attack, it drops the attacking data packets straightaway. This method can sometimes be counterproductive, but it is the safest way to go. Alternatively, the IPS can deal with suspicious traffic by limiting the traffic's bandwidth. This can be done when the traffic is suspicious with a lesser degree of confidence. The traffic may be undesirable, but, this way, it should not overload the network.

Choosing IDS or IPS

IDS and IPS use similar techniques for identifying attacks, and IPS has the added feature of attack prevention. But IPS, due to this added advantage and requirement of more hardware & software resources, is typically more expensive than IDS. So, what security system should network or system administrators buy? The following points can make the decision easier.

Threat spectrum factors

- *Network size and type of data stored*: Different networks function in different environments with different threat spectrums. A network with a limited number of clients and less-sensitive data has a reduced threat spectrum than a network hosting services for a huge client base with critical data storage, like credit card information. Bigger networks with more resources need added protection, so, for them, an IPS is the better choice.

- *DoS attack threat level*: Networks used by businesses with growing competitive markets are more liable to DoS attacks, but, fortunately, IDS/IPS techniques are very effective against these types of attacks. Therefore, networks used by growing organizations should not take a risk when it comes to network security; these networks should use IPS to prevent the DoS attack before it happens.

Upgrade potential

Many vendors provide both IDP and IPS systems, meaning that an IDS by one vendor, once observed and deemed effective, can often later be upgraded to an IPS from the same vendor.

Administration staff skills

Both IDSs and IPSs are very complex machines requiring expertise to maintain and operate. If the correct arrangement of support professionals is unavailable, operating the IDS/IPS can be a nightmare. The most effective security techniques combine technology, procedures, and skilled personnel.

Compare cost and requirements

Aside from the initial cost, IDSs and IPSs accrue installation, maintenance, and operations costs. A network administrator should evaluate the network's requirements, in terms of security and incident response, as a major deciding factor for whether to get an IDS or an IPS.

For example, if a network requires forensics, analysis, and more network visibility, then it would likely be better equipped with IDS. However, if the network is more prone to attacks due to the nature of the threat paradigm, it should use an IPS.

Intrusion systems, like all other security hardware and software mechanisms discussed so far, are employed to serve a network by safeguarding against security threats to network resources. If a network is hosting sensitive, time-critical, system, or classified data, or if the network comes under the purview of severe compliance conventions, then the organization should seriously consider using an IDS, an IPS, or both. Reviewing the examples in this chapter can help network administrators determine the relevant network benefits available from intrusion detection and prevention systems.

CHAPTER

Virtual Private Networks

What is a Virtual Private Network (VPN)?

With the growth of networks and related technologies, users' reliance on network-based services and automation has been increasing daily.

The foundation of any network is its infrastructure. Since wireless infrastructure has a limited range of operation in terms of distance as well as bandwidth, many network administrators rely heavily on wired networks to connect sites, offices, and clients around the globe. But, how could a network administrator lay wired network infrastructure all around the globe or maintain it on a constant basis? It would require too much money and staff to lay, maintain, and manage so much network infrastructure.

Many multinational organizations solve this problem through use of the biggest, most public network available: the Internet. In a typical scenario, site offices and head offices have their own internal LANs, and these individual LANs are connected to each other through the Internet. But public networks, like the Internet, are usually too insecure to be used for corporate communications. Perhaps the best solution to this problem is the *virtual private network*.

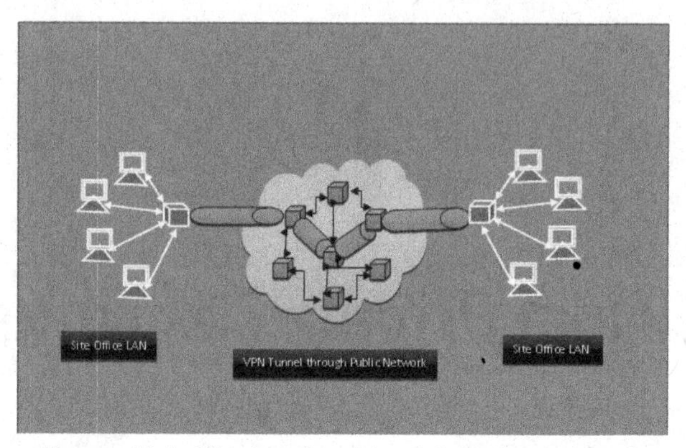

Figure 11.1. Site-to-site virtual private network

A *virtual private network*, or *VPN*, is a secure channel or a network that carries data transmissions over an otherwise insecure network. The secure channel can be between two end points, like a tunnel, or among more than two points, like another network. It is often an extension of a secure network over an insecure network, such as the public Internet. A VPN is also called a tunnel or tunneling, indicating a notion of secure passage through open country.

Going a little further, VPN tunnels are used for transmission of private data (data to be exposed within an organization only) through a public network, such as the Internet, in such a way that the transmission is not exposed to or realized by the underlying public network nodes or routers. This kind of tunneling is achieved by encapsulating the private data in the public network's transmission units. This chapter explains the process in more detail.

VPN scenarios

A VPN is typically established in one of two scenarios.

Site-to-site VPN typically involves creating a connection between two geographically separated sites of the same organization. The organization relies on the Internet to communicate data between the two sites. So, from both ends, the organization pays for sufficient Internet bandwidth, depending on the amount of traffic. Then, the connection, or *VPN tunnel*, is configured between the main routers/gateways of both sites' LANs, allowing users on one side of the tunnel to send data to and receive data from other side with little or no concern about the insecurity of the public network infrastructure in between.

Remote access VPN establishes a VPN tunnel between a gateway and an individual computer system. Remote access VPN is normally required when a user needs access to network resources or services from far away. In this scenario, one side is a network and the other is a single host. Therefore, a VPN tunnel is established between a router/gateway and a remote host. This enables the remote computer user to send and receive emails, files, and services to and from the network.

VPN Protocols

There are many ways of establishing VPNs. This section introduces four:

- Point-to-point tunneling protocol (PPTP)
- Layer 2 tunneling protocol (L2TP)
- IPSec protocol
- Secure socket layer protocol (SSL)

Point-to-point tunneling protocol (PPTP)

Point-to-point tunneling protocol (*PPTP*) allows remote users to access the main network through a VPN tunnel using *point-to-point protocol* (*PPP*). PPP can help establish a data communication channel between two hosts, providing authentication, encryption, and compression features. This used to be a very popular way of accessing the Internet on dial-up through *Internet service providers* (*ISPs*).

Layer 2 tunneling protocol (L2TP)

Layer 2 tunneling protocol (*L2TP*) is a further extension of PPTP and another protocol, called *layer 2 forwarding protocol* (*L2F*). Like PPTP, L2TP was created to connect to ISPs and obtain Internet services. Also like PPTP, L2TP does not provide encryption and confidentiality unless some other protocol is used alongside it to provide encryption, authentication, and integrity.

IPSec protocol

IPSec is a widely used protocol for modern-day VPNs. It is a highly flexible, complex, and comprehensive protocol, addressing various options and techniques. While such complexity may initially seem intimidating, the flexibility and elaborate mechanisms for setting up secure communications should more than make up for it.

IPSec provides strong mechanisms for encryption, authentication, and integrity. It is normally used to establish site-to-site VPNs, but it can also be used for remote access VPNs. IPSec's flexibility comes from its open and modular framework, allowing other assisting protocols to be employed according to the network administrator's needs and decisions regarding which features to use and which to remove or ignore.

IPSec uses two basic security protocols: *authentication header* (*AH*) *protocol* and *encapsulation payload* (*ESP*) *protocol*. As the names suggests, AH focuses on authentication, whereas ESP provides encryption to improve integrity checks and confidentiality.

IPSec can be utilized in two modes of operation.

Transport mode emphasizes security in the OSI layers above the IP layer.[39] It focuses on the *IP payload*—the data regarding upper

---

[39] Refer to Figure 8.1.

layers—which is how it was given the name *transport mode*. Transport mode of IPSec is employed when there is a requirement to establish a VPN between two hosts, such as a computer system and a server, or between two computer systems. As it focuses on the IP payload, the original IP header remains intact throughout the traffic path followed by the packets.

By contrast, *tunnel mode* is used for establishing VPNs between gateways/routers, and not directly between hosts. In tunnel mode, the complete IP packet is encapsulated in the new IPSec packet, which is not removed by the routers on the transmission path. This allows the complete original IP packet to travel all the way from one end (gateway) to another end (again, a gateway) without being exposed to the network in between. The added benefit of tunnel mode is that a VPN established between two routers enables the host computers behind the routers on both sides to communicate with each other securely, without the need to implement IPSec on them individually.

Both transport mode and tunnel mode have strengths and weaknesses. Transport mode, although it provides end-to-end security between hosts, would require implementation on each node individually in order to create VPNs from all the clients on a network to another site. On the other hand, tunnel mode is a very cost-effective way of establishing VPNs between gateways, removing the need for individual implementations on clients. Therefore, transport mode is only suited for a remote user accessing network resources and services, while tunnel mode can be used for site-to-site VPNs.

IPSec VPNs have several benefits, all generally due to the fact that they are VPNs established at layer 3 (network layer).[40] Since the VPN is layer-3-based, users are neither required to know that the VPN is being used nor do they need to do anything for it to properly function; as far as they are concerned, the IPSec VPN is completely

[40] Refer to Figure 8.1.

invisible. An IPSec VPN's layer 3 operation enables it to monitor and secure all network traffic, both incoming and outgoing. Unlike other types of VPNs, an IPSec VPN is totally independent of an application running over it. Finally, IPSec VPNs are very well-suited to secure communication between sites, as the hassle of implementation at each individual computer system is avoided.

The basic steps for establishing an IPSec VPN between two computer systems are:

- A computer system requests an IPSec connection to another computer system.
- A handshake occurs between the two sides to determine various configuration settings, like the cryptographic algorithm.[41]
- Both systems set up a *security association* for this connection. A security association is a set of metadata records of a single IPSec connection's configuration settings.
- The systems start communicating securely using IPSec, based on the already set-up security association for the connection.

Secure socket layer (SSL) protocol

Secure socket layer (*SSL*), unlike IPSec, is a transport-layer protocol, or, more specifically, SSL works between the session and transport layers (layers 5 and 4).[42] SSL is typically used in conjunction with other VPN protocols to provide excellent security with simplicity and speed. The most common way SSL is seen today is *HTTP over SSL*, also called *HTTPS* or *HTTP secure*, using SSL's public key and data encryption abilities, as illustrated in Figure 11.2.[43]

---

[41] Refer to Chapter 7 for a discussion about cryptographic algorithms in greater depth.

[42] Refer to Figure 8.1.

[43] Refer to Chapter 7 for discussion of public keys and data encryption.

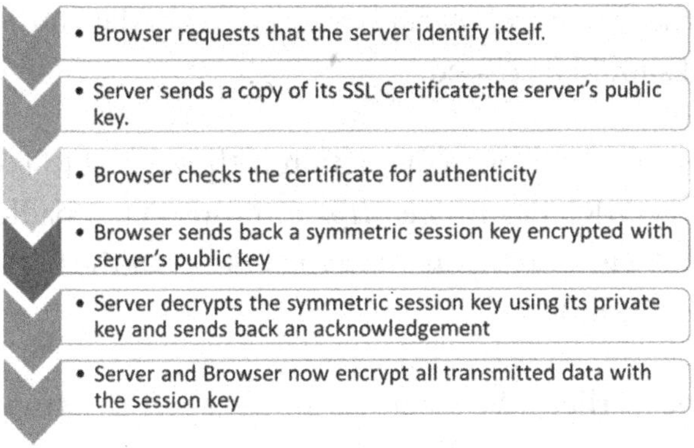

- Browser requests that the server identify itself.
- Server sends a copy of its SSL Certificate;the server's public key.
- Browser checks the certificate for authenticity
- Browser sends back a symmetric session key encrypted with server's public key
- Server decrypts the symmetric session key using its private key and sends back an acknowledgement
- Server and Browser now encrypt all transmitted data with the session key

Figure 11.2: HTTP over SSL (HTTPS)

When a user accesses a website, that website may have both secure and public portions. When the user goes from a public page on the website to a secure page, the web server will start the necessary tasks to invoke SSL, require the user to be authenticated in some fashion, and protect this type of communication.

To start establishing the secure channel, the server sends a message back to the user, indicating a secure session should be established, and the user, in response, sends its security parameters. The server compares those security parameters to its own until it finds a match. The server authenticates the user by sending it a digital certificate, and, if the user decides to trust the server, the process continues. The server can require the user to send over a digital certificate for mutual authentication, but that is rare. The user generates a session key and encrypts it with the server's public key.[44] This encrypted key is sent to the web server, and both server and user utilize this symmetric key to encrypt the data they send back and forth.

SSL keeps the communication path open until one of the parties requests to end the session. The session is usually ended when the

[44] Refer to Chapter 7 for a deeper discussion regarding public and private keys.

user sends the server an *FIN packet*—a packet of data indicating that the channel should be closed.

Users can verify whether a connection is through HTTPS or not by looking at the URL bar to see *https://.* Moreover, a padlock or key icon is usually visible either behind the URL or at the bottom corner of the browser window.

As discussed earlier, SSL operates in between the transport and session layers. However, HTTP is an application-layer protocol.[45] With HTTPS, HTTP is actually functioning on top of SSL, which is why it is called HTTP over SSL. HTTPS is just one example where SSL provides an added layer of security to an application-layer protocol; SSL can provide security to other upper-layer protocols as well.

Comparing IPSec and SSL

Since IPSec and SSL are the most widely used protocols for establishing VPNs, it would be pertinent to make a clear and concise comparison between them.

- IPSec is a highly complex suite of standards with the built-in flexibility of adding or removing any functionality offered. It caters to all the requirements for establishing a secure VPN, but, at the same time, it does not require the implementer to use all its provisions.
- For cryptographic protection of the data being sent or received in the VPN tunnel, IPSec has added protection in terms of the strength of the algorithm.
- IPSec operates at layer 3 (network layer), and SSL operates at layer 4 (transport layer). This gives IPSec an edge over SSL, as SSL has to be implemented for different applications separately, whereas IPSec protection guards all of the layers above it.

[45] Refer to Figure 8.1.

The comparison described above is presented in Table 11.1 for further clarity.

IPSec	Criteria	SSL
High	**Complexity**	Low
Very flexible	**Flexibility**	Limited
Excellent	**Cryptographic Security**	Good
Available	**Central Management**	No
Layer 3 (Network)	**OSI Layer**	Layer 4 (Transport)
Transport & Tunnel	**Operational Modes**	None
Transparently	**Protection to Upper Layers**	Needs separate Implementation

Table 11.1: Comparing IPSec and SSL

VPN Advantages and Disadvantages

VPNs are very common today, due to their utility in securing data communications over the Internet. While the primary advantage of a VPN is the ability to use a public network, like the Internet, rather than expend the necessary costs and labor to establish a private, long-haul network infrastructure, VPNs also have several other advantages and disadvantages.

Advantages

- VPNs significantly reduce connectivity costs for widely spread offices or employees.
- If VPNs are established precisely with security in mind, the need for leased lines is eliminated.
- VPNs create fewer hassles, limited coordination requirements, and a comparatively smaller cost—the only recurring cost to be paid is broadband connectivity.

- The initial configuration may not be very simple, but, after it has been set once, there is hardly any maintenance overhead.

Disadvantages

- In spite of security precautions, VPNs still operate through a public network, meaning they are not ideal for transferring sensitive information.
- VPNs can provide remote users with privileged access to an internal network. Misuse of this access can prove devastating if there is a security breach or compromise.
- IPSec VPNs and NAT[46] can have conflicts if not configured properly.
- Due to typical configuration settings, VPN traffic is often not visible to an intrusion detection system (IDS).[47]
- VPNs are prone to man-in-the-middle attacks.[48]
- VPNs typically do not have a secure default configuration, which can lead to an unexpected security breach.

---

[46] Refer to Chapter 9 for more about NAT.

[47] Refer to Chapter 10 for more about IDS.

[48] Refer to Chapter 8 for more about MITM attacks.

CHAPTER

Data Backup and Recovery

In computer security, the question is rarely *if* an attack will happen, but *when*. Even the most formidable defenses can be breached. Therefore, measures to safeguard critical assets and curtail damage in case of a breach are important aspects of information and computer security.

Users should assume that one day an attacker may reach the internal network, break the password, or carry out the cryptanalysis of a cipher. So how do users minimize the amount of damage? What would be the best way to mitigate these risks?

Importance of Data

Once an attacker has breached the outer perimeter, such as border firewalls, what could be corrupted or compromised to cause the most damage? The most critical resource in a system, without any doubt, is the data.

Software applications can always be redeployed and configured to default, and system services can be restored to normal after an attack or a natural disaster. However, data is always changing. Users constantly create new files, make changes to existing ones, move files around, etc. So, an attack or natural disaster that destroys some or all of the data becomes a nightmare if data cannot be restored because precautionary measures were not previously taken.

For example, when a computer crashes and is no longer working, the biggest trouble is not re-installing the operating system or all of the application software or redoing the configuration settings. The most devastating loss is the data, such as documents, personal photos, videos, etc. The problem increases in complexity with the size of the data.

Defining Data Backup and Recovery

A *data backup* is simply making one or more copies of data. Simple examples include making regular copies of important files, like office documents, family photos, and videos, or even the complete hard disk.

Data backup can be further understood by thinking about its utility—why backup is needed or when will it be used. Merely creating a data backup might not be enough of a precaution.

Need for backups and recovery

Users should always consider backups and recovery mechanisms, even if they never actually have to use them. Backups and recovery mechanisms are useful in the context of the following scenarios:

- *Hardware failure*: It is not uncommon for hardware, including critical devices such a database machine, to stop working without any apparent cause.
- *User factors*: Even the best administrators and professionals can make devastating mistakes—for example, deleting a folder that was actually a customer record by mistake. Also, a frustrated employee could delete or modify important data on purpose.
- *Unpredictable natural calamities*: Earthquakes, fires, floods, etc. can be unpredictable and may cause irreparable damage to users' resources.

- *Enemy actions*: General malware attacks, targeted hacking, or even terrorist attacks may lead to destruction or corruption of all or a portion of data.

Importance of data backup location

The data backup has to be used for recovering the data in case the original data is lost. Therefore, the backed-up data must be strategically placed with the worst-case scenario in mind:

> User X, while working late at the office one night, thinks it is appropriate to keep a backup copy of his office work on a USB flash drive. While creating the backup, X kept in mind the possibilities of a crash or hardware failure and loss of the data kept on the computer. The next morning, when X goes in to the office, he realizes his laptop has been stolen. Unfortunately, in the carrying bag with the laptop was also the USB flash drive containing the backup. X lost the original data along with the backup data. However, if the disaster had only been a laptop failure, the backup could have helped.

The above example shows that the mere act of backing up data brings only some advantages; the location of the data backup is another important aspect to consider. The purpose of data backup is fulfilled only when the original data can be recovered in case of loss. A data backup that is lost with the original data is of no use.

Figure 12.1 displays a few possible options for backup data locations. For each location, an example is provided of a disaster scenario under which that particular backup could be conveniently used.

Notably, for each disaster scenario in the figure, the previous backup location may not be able to recover the data. When deciding on a location for data backup, users should keep in mind the scenarios that they are likely to encounter. Other considerations in deciding a backup location are the probability of a disaster's occurrence, the importance of the data, and a cost-benefit analysis.

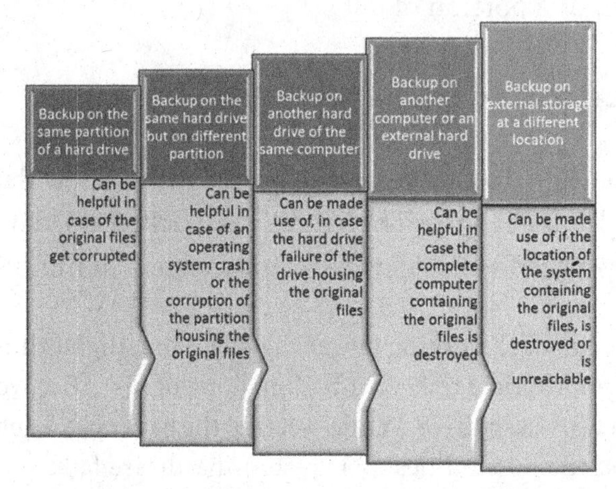

Figure 12.1: Backup locations and their implications on recovery

Amount of data backup

No user wants to think about losing a single file of data. The solution is to create backups in a way that a complete copy of critical data would always be available. Such backup strategies include:

- *Full backup*: As the name says, this is a complete backup of all of the data. As more data is created, the size of backup increases; so, too, does the time required to update such backups.
- *Incremental backup*: An incremental backup backs up only changed data. That means the data backup process is configured to update the backup only with data from a designated start point to its latest state. This kind of backup is convenient in terms of time duration and speed but difficult to manage because it requires maintaining backups of different time durations.
- *Differential backup*: Differential backups are an intelligent backup strategy; data is backed up from the point of last full backup to the present. The total size of the backup increases

with the amount of time since the last full backup, as does the time required to create the backup.

Frequency of data backup

How often should data be backed up? This is another important and relevant question. What factors dictate this decision? Before discussing the possibilities, consider the following example:

> An organization has a policy of maintaining a complete backup of its data on an external tape drive. The drive is placed in a site away from the actual system. However, the backup is only updated every two weeks. If a disaster hits the original data in between the updates, the data that was created or altered after the last backup would be lost.

Backup frequency should match the frequency of data creation or modification and the amount of data loss users can presumably sustain. Backup frequency strategies include:

- *Daily full backup*: In this strategy, a user may choose to take a full backup of all data every day at a set time. This may become very time-consuming as more data is added on a daily basis. The storage media used for the daily full backup may remain the same, and every day, the data is written over the earlier backup. There may be some extra storage devices to keep a few old backups.
- *Once or rare full backup and daily incremental backup*: In this strategy, users create a full backup only once, or rarely, and then create daily incremental backups. This way, if the original data is lost, a full recovery can be made using the full backup and the increments. However, more time between full backups means more incremental backups, increasing the time needed for recovery.
- *Weekly or monthly full backup and daily differential backup*: This is a variation of the last strategy, but it replaces incremental

backup with differential backup. This will reduce the storage media requirement, since the same storage media can be used for daily differential backups. However, over time, the size of the differential backup will grow and so will the time required to create the backup.

- *Monthly full backup, weekly differential backup, and daily incremental backup*: This is arguably the best backup strategy. After creating a full backup, the user creates daily incremental backups and, by the end of the week, creates a differential backup of the complete week from the full backup. Thereafter, the incremental backups should again be on a daily basis from the time of last differential backup. In this way, the size of incremental backups will not grow too much over time. Differential backups can be an added advantage alongside full backups.

Storage media used for data backup

The storage media used for the backup is yet another important decision users must consider when putting backup and recovery mechanisms into action. Different types of storage media are available and commonly used today, including magnetic tapes, hard disks, optical storage, and solid state storage. The following considerations are important when determining the correct storage media for your backup strategy:

- *Reliability*: Even though the days of floppy disks and CD drives have passed, some users still insist on storing important data on a floppy disk—then complaining when they are unable to recover everything. A backup that is not recoverable after a disaster is worse than no backup at all.

  Backup media are usually written and overwritten many times. The storage device is often moved from one place to another physically. The media chosen should not be prone to errors and loss of information. Therefore, the reliability of storage media should be the most important factor when deciding on the type of backup media.

- *Data writing speed*: While data writing speed may not be a matter of concern for users with only a few gigabytes of data, it can be of great concern for users with multiple terabytes of data. The data backup process, if it takes too much time, can add costs of labor, effort, and time.
- *Data reading speed*: When a backup is created, the data is written in large, sequential chunks. However, when reading all or a portion of the data, to check or copy it, reading speed becomes important. The hardware, the physical structure, the data-holding mechanism (magnetic, electrical, or optical), and the difference between sequential and random access ability will all affect data reading and writing speed. For example, when copying a portion of data from the backup, random access ability will result in faster copying operations.

What is Data Recovery?

Closely linked to data backup is data recovery. A data backup that cannot be recovered is useless.

Data recovery mechanisms cannot be isolated from data backup mechanisms. Without backups, one cannot think of recovery. However, recovery procedures and mechanisms themselves are also very important. Without a proper recovery mechanism, even a good data backup cannot be utilized fully.

Data recovery from a healthy backup is not a difficult task, but choosing when to recover the system from a data backup is an important decision. There is a dire need for comprehensive data backup and recovery mechanisms to be placed in line with the overall backup and recovery policy put into action by responsible security or network administrators.

For example, in the event of loss of data on a running system, first, the health state of the available data backup must be checked and certified by concerned team. Second, the correct type of data backup needed for recovery should be identified, especially since the extent of damage may only necessitate a recovery from an incremental or differential backup. After completing the recovery process, responsible administrators must certify that the recovered data is correct and complete by checking the data thoroughly.

Business Continuity Plan (BCP)

A *business continuity plan* (*BCP*) keeps the processes and the functionality of a system up and running to perform intended tasks, in the event of a disaster. A BCP allows organizations to survive and keep providing critical services, despite natural and human-inflicted disasters.

A BCP includes more than data recovery; it also covers the recovery of data, services, and resources necessary for the organization to remain as functional as before the disaster. To save costs, the BCP may aim only to provide uninterrupted critical services while accepting some delay in less critical services.

BCP benefits

Benefits of having a ready BCP include:

- Faster disaster recovery, with less chaos and confusion
- Easier disaster survival, with a better chance for recovery
- No legal complications from loss of data and break in services
- Potential insurance premium reduction
- Potential credit rating improvement
- Increased customer confidence

Steps in formulating a BCP

The steps to build and test a BCP are sequential and logical. These steps include:

- *Risk assessment*: First and foremost, businesses should think of scenarios that may hurt or slow down system and network processes. These scenarios should be as close to the actual environment as possible. These threat scenarios form the basis of a risk mitigation plan.
- *Business impact analysis*: Each threat scenario and its associated risks, along with mitigation strategies, are evaluated in detail to determine impact on the business. At this stage, the threat scenarios should be prioritized based on potential business impact.
- *Disaster recovery plan*: Next, the business prepares a disaster recovery plan with threats and possibilities in mind.
- *BCP development*: With the disaster recovery plan in place, the organization should know what services would be needed immediately after a disaster. Without those services, the whole organization's functionality would be in jeopardy. A BCP should be developed with the need of such important services in mind.
- *Documentation*: A security team, in consultation with the executives, should document both the disaster recovery plan and the BCP so that the plans are readily available when needed.
- *Testing*: Regular security audits should include checking the disaster recovery plan and the BCP. Even if no audit is carried out, both plans should undergo periodic testing and review.
- *Updates*: Emerging threats, changing needs, additional resources, and growing network infrastructure are just some of the reasons why the disaster recovery plan and BCP should be updated often. It is recommended that the cycle of testing and updating the disaster recovery plan and the BCP

be conducted both periodically and with every change in a threat scenario or significant change in resources.

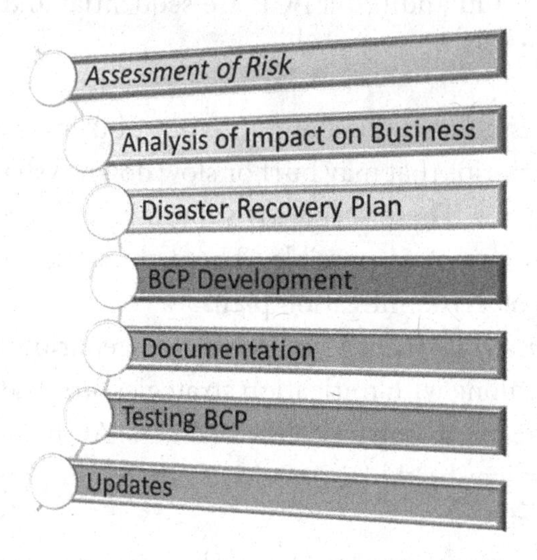

Figure 12.2: Steps for Formulating a BCP

CHAPTER

13

Cloud Computing

What is Cloud Computing?

Cloud computing is when users lease data storage, processing power, applications, or other services from a location accessible through the Internet. Users can then access the data and applications hosted online (known in this context as *the cloud*) without needing to install any applications, run programs, or store data on local computer systems. All of the data and applications are powered by and served from the cloud.

The awareness of and attention given to cloud computing has grown in today's increasingly global environment. Users can be quick to view cloud computing as a means to dramatically decrease computing costs while also increasing productivity, but they overlook the potential security risks linked with cloud computing. This chapter explains what cloud computing is, how it can reduce costs while increasing productivity, and some of the underlying threats and vulnerabilities of cloud computing.

It might be helpful to first understand the history and evolution of cloud computing, especially when compared with other computing architectures, before addressing some of the specific advantages offered by cloud computing.

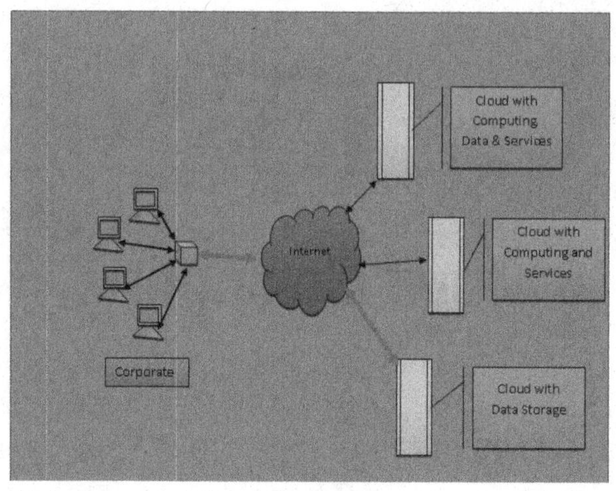

Figure 13.1: A corporation utilizing data storage from a cloud

History of cloud computing

A good place to start examining the history of cloud computing is *mainframe architecture*—several dumb terminals connected to a single powerful computer called a *mainframe. Dumb terminals*, or *thin clients*, are extremely basic computer systems with no local processing power or data storage. A mainframe computer and dumb terminals are locally connected, rather than connected through the Internet.

With the passage of time, processing and storage became less costly, and the rise of personal computers with their own CPUs, hard disk storage, and, perhaps most importantly, connectivity via the Internet led to a new type of architecture: *client-server architecture*. Now, with an Internet connection, a standalone computer system could easily access services, data, and processing power from servers around the world.

Cloud computing has combined benefits of mainframe and client-server architecture. Like mainframe architecture, cloud computing relies on terminals, but these terminals are often *thick clients*—full computer systems with their own processing power and data storage, though they are still considered very basic when compared with the cloud's resources. Using thick clients allows the machines to work on their own when they are required to do so, but they can also utilize the cloud's resources when they are connected to Internet. Users are not required to use the same terminal or computer system every time to access the cloud; they can access it from anywhere.

Advantages of cloud computing

Cloud computing offers many advantages when compared with its predecessors, mainframe architecture and client-server architecture. These advantages include:

- *Disaster recovery*: When users fully rely on cloud computing (i.e., all their computing, data storage, and application services reside on the cloud), only their terminals need to be managed. This means that the work of those users—or an entire organization—is not dependent on the location of offices. Even if the terminals not working, the employees can work from home or some other location. The users will not need to take precautions against threats of data loss or a break in services during a disaster. This is because the cloud service providers themselves normally employ elaborate business continuity plans (BCPs) in order to provide uninterrupted cloud services.[49]
- *Economy*: Users relying on cloud computing have no need to invest heavily in infrastructure, such as processing power, network capabilities, servers, and even high-end computers systems, since thin clients or *smart clients*[50] can be used instead.

[49] Refer to Chapter 12 for more about BCPs.

[50] Smart clients are in between thin and thick clients. They have do not have much storage, processing power, or RAM. Since they have their own resources, they make use of cloud resources but perform better than thin clients.

- *Reliability*: Cloud service providers, due to nature of their business, invest heavily to make sure their systems are reliable. They normally have excellent disaster recovery plans and BCPs and ensure their data centers are established to provide high availability and redundancy for all of their services.
- *Data loss protection*: Users do not have to worry about data theft or loss due to a breakdown when all of the data is at cloud storage. Even if a terminal or computer system is stolen, no data would actually be lost.
- *No wasted resources*: Under normal circumstances, users spend more on computer equipment than they initially anticipated. For example if a user needs increased data, the next size up could be so massive that it wouldn't totally be consumed for years. Underutilized resources can be a serious, wasteful cost. But in the case of cloud computing, users pay only for the resources they actually use. There is no need to buy extra storage just in case it is needed later because when more storage is required, users can buy exactly the amount they need from the cloud storage provider.
- *Additional resources are quickly available*: In a cloud computing scenario, users can access additional resources almost immediately after purchase, rather than needing to wait for hardware or software to be shipped, assembled, and/or installed.

Cloud Computing Models

Cloud computing can be classified into three models:

- Software as a service (SaaS)
- Platform as a service (PaaS)
- Infrastructure as a service (IaaS)

Figure 13.2: Cloud computing models

Software as a service (SaaS)

Software as a service (*SaaS*) cloud computing relies on the cloud provider to deliver application services. The services are accessed by users, usually directly from a web browser, with no required installations or downloads, except, perhaps, a software *plugin* (an extension to add some specific feature to an existing application program).

With SaaS, users no longer have to install and run application software on each and every computer. Since the software applications remain in the custody and ownership of the cloud provider's servers, no installation at individual machines is required. The machines only have to connect to the cloud to access the software applications.

SaaS is the most common cloud computing model; many users use SaaS without even knowing that they are using cloud services. Examples include healthcare applications, email collaboration, and customer relationship management.

Platform as a service (PaaS)

Some users may choose to utilize a cloud platform for their own applications/services. A *platform* is a major piece of software, such as an operating system, operating environment, or a database, under which various smaller application programs can be designed to run.

Users who choose *platform as a service* (*PaaS*) get a reliable framework they can use to develop and customize their own applications. The development process, testing mechanisms, and application deployment are faster, easier, and more economical. This is because PaaS reduces the amount of necessary coding, automates business functions, and assists in migrating applications to a hybrid model of both a private and a public or commercial cloud.

Infrastructure as a service (IaaS)

Infrastructure as a service (*IaaS*) provides users access only to the cloud provider's infrastructure. In the IT sense, *infrastructure* refers to data-center-like capabilities, such as computing power, storage, internal network, etc. Users can then build their own architectural frameworks or platforms and develop their own software applications on top. This allows users to start almost from scratch—but with the significant boost provided by data center infrastructure. The cloud provider manages the servers, network, storage, necessary power, disaster recovery plan, and BCP for the infrastructure. The users are responsible for the development environment, O&M of software, and issuance of new releases.

Cloud Computing and Security

Cloud service providers are responsible for their own security. Thus the cloud services are as secure as the provider chooses to make them. Users dependent on an external cloud face very different security dynamics than they would if they were controlling their own security.

Areas of concern

The main questions users should ask when adopting cloud computing or selecting a cloud provider should include:

- Can the provider be trusted with hosting confidential data and critical systems?
- Do the cloud provider's services meet industry standards and international best practices?
    - Are they certified through an auditor?
    - Will they allow user visits for peace of mind?

- Does the provider have requisite experience handling needs similar to the user's?
    - Is a secure environment and information assurance offered?
    - Are resources sufficient for security needs?

Cloud computing security threats

We will now look at a brief list of threats to cloud computing delivery models, based on several of the security foundations.[51]

- *Confidentiality*: The threat to confidentiality increases when more stakeholders or partners are involved. Confidentiality can be threatened by data leakage or threats from *insiders* (either authorized users or cloud provider employees), due to improperly configured access rights, or from outside threats, such as a remote attack to the cloud service or platform or a remote hardware attack on the cloud infrastructure. Even the possibility of a social engineering attack by outsiders can have devastating effects on confidentiality. [52]

[51] Refer to Chapter 1 to recap the different security foundations.

[52] Social engineering is explored in greater depth in Chapter 15.

- *Integrity*: Cloud providers supplying many different users with data storage can lead to increased threats to data integrity, such as data segregation issues or vulnerabilities; poor, unintentional, or faulty access control mechanisms; or faulty hardware isolation.
- *Availability*: A cloud provider continuously manages the requests of many users at a time. These requests include subscription changes, resource increases, and data storage size modification. Incorrectly managing these requests can increase the risks of threat to availability.
    - **Denial of Service (DoS):** DoS attacks can affect cloud providers, even if they have sophisticated and elaborate countermeasures in place. With enhancements in technology, attackers are also gaining advantages, such as using their own cloud services to make DoS a success.
    - **Physical disruption:** Either a natural or human-inflicted disaster could be catastrophic for a cloud provider and would certainly affect users.

Important tips for cloud computing data security

Users deciding to adopt cloud computing should take precautionary measures to ensure the safety of their data.

- Users relying on cloud data storage should know the location where their data is actually stored; otherwise, they cannot be sure of their data security. Users should also be aware of what happens to their data when the contract with the cloud services provider is terminated.
- Even when using cloud storage, users should always back up their most critical data.[53] An even better precautionary measure is to not host critical data with the cloud provider at all.

---

[53] See Chapter 12 for data backup and recovery strategies.

- Users must be sure that the safety of their data is equally important to the cloud provider. Users should not only know the location of their data; they should also review the security measures being taken by the cloud provider to protect the data. When creating a cloud computing model and searching for a provider, it is a good idea to consult with providers' existing clients. That may give a better insight into each cloud provider's strengths and weaknesses than asking the cloud providers directly.
- Users should be sure to test their own data security. Although the cloud provider should be testing its own security processes through audits, users should perform their own tests as well. Users can consider hiring an ethical hacker to do penetration testing for additional certainty regarding the secure custody of their data.

No system can claim to have absolute security, but cloud computing has traditionally done a very good job. However, as cloud computing becomes more popular and widespread, it is also becoming more vulnerable to security threats.

CHAPTER

Physical Security and Biometrics

Physical security is equally as important as technical security and should always be a top priority. In cases of unauthorized access, the problem almost always lies with physical security issues. This chapter discusses physical security and relevant techniques, including biometrics.

What is Physical Security?

Physical security means the measures taken to protect information technology (IT) system resources, like hardware, software, and network devices, from external dangers, including fire, water, theft, short-circuiting, etc. Physical security could be considered of even greater importance than technical security measures. Most, if not all, IT resources reside within a physical site; the setting around and within this site should be protected from unwelcome events.

Breach of physical security can compromise the availability or confidentiality security foundations—or both.[54] Examples include:

- A natural disaster, like a flood or earthquake, destroys a data center and affects the availability of services.

[54] Refer to Chapter 1 for a discussion of the seven security foundations.

- A break-in at a data center or theft of a server creates confidentiality and availability compromises.
- A careless administrator spills a cup of coffee on a server machine, leading to non-availability of services.

Goals of physical security for IT setup

Physical security does not only apply to IT, but rather to all of a user's resources. Keeping in mind the concerns related to information and computer security, the goals of IT physical security include:

- *No unauthorized access*, especially to areas where secure IT is kept, such as a data center or server room.
- *Protection against any damage to or theft of the IT resources* with a defense plan, including proactive and reactive countermeasures against sabotage activities, terrorist attacks, theft, and other carefully examined threat scenarios. For example, to prevent a short circuit in the server room, proactive measures would include ensuring good electric wiring, installing fire alarms and fire extinguishers, and practicing drills.
- *Keeping personal and professional IT separate* to avoid the security issues that can be created by bringing personal hardware to work. For example, an employee might bring in a USB flash drive and copy data to take home and work on it, with good intentions. But if the computer the employee uses does not have the proper security measures, data could be lost. Similarly, a rogue employee could use a personal storage device to bring and inject malware into the company's network. These two scenarios might seem remote, but they are actual real-world examples of events that have happened and can happen when employees are allowed to mix personal and work IT.

Physical security policies and mechanisms

Physical security is often maintained by a combination of policies and mechanisms based on access control, monitoring, and surveillance.[55] Such mechanisms include:

- Guards monitoring points of entry and exit
- Photo ID cards for all persons allowed to enter, which could include color-coding the cards to specify permissions for access to particular areas
- Magnetic, RFID, or biometric cards for entering sensitive areas
- Surveillance cameras at sensitive areas to monitor activities and generate alarms
- Turnstiles and barriers
- Metal detectors and walk-through gates
- Electric fencing
- Automatic locks and keys
- Burglar alarm systems
- Biometric access control

Biometric Techniques

Several of the previously mentioned physical security policies and mechanisms included references to biometrics. *Biometrics* is the measurement and analysis of a person's biological parameters for identification. Biometric techniques are not the only means to implement physical security, but they are some of the best, as their methods have continued to improve and their usage has continued to grow. The main difference between biometrics and other access control technologies is that access control has typically been concerned with identifying users based of what they possessed, such as a password. Biometric technology identifies users based on what they are, or, more specifically, some intrinsic physical or behavioral trait.

[55] Refer to Chapter 3 for a discussion on access control.

General mechanisms of a biometric system

All biometric systems typically work the same way. First, in the *enrollment phase*, the specific biometric property is scanned or otherwise read, preprocessed for noise reduction, and stored in a database. Then, when the time comes for the *recognition phase*, an access control check is performed using a similar sensor to that used for the initial recording to capture the specific biometric property of the user seeking to enter and compare it with the information already present in the database. If a match occurs, the person is allowed to proceed. If there is no match, an alert is generated.

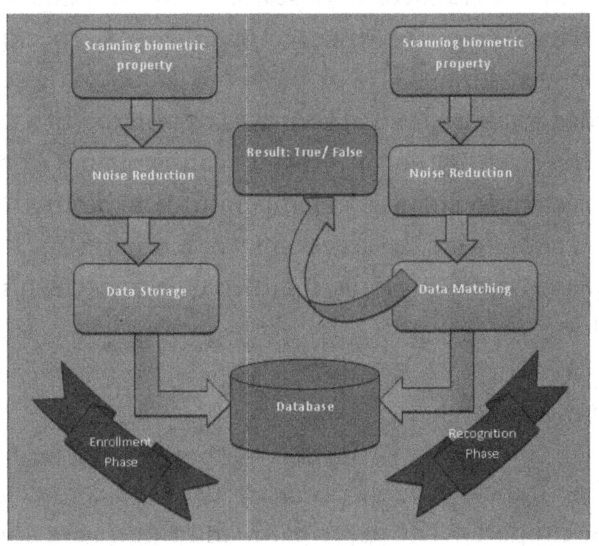

Figure 14.1: Biometric access control system

Biometric Techniques against Static Properties

The basic idea behind biometric technology is to use some unique biological characteristic of human beings that some mechanism can use to identify users. The following unique characteristics have often been used by biometric technology, based on unique, unchanging, individual properties.

Fingerprinting

Fingerprinting is perhaps the oldest and most-employed biometric technique. It used to be that ink was used to get one or more of a person's fingerprint patterns in order to confirm identity. Nowadays, digital fingerprint scanners are commonly employed. The user places the finger(s) on an optical reader; the fingerprint information is scanned and compared against the recorded fingerprints in the database; and, if there is a match, the biometric system grants the user access.

Fingerprinting provides convenient access control, due to its speed and simplicity, especially when compared with checking photo ID cards or providing a PIN or password (though those methods may be added as an additional security layer on top of a fingerprint scanner). However, if the fingerprint scanner is not good quality or is not resistant to changes in temperature or the environment, it may further complicate the access control mechanisms. Fingerprint scanners also require periodic maintenance and cleaning to stay functional.

Hand geometry

As the name indicates, *hand geometry* uses the complete hand as a biometric property. The user's palm and fingers are aligned on a metal surface with guidance pegs, and a scanner then reads the hand and finger attributes and compares the data to the hand geometry parameters in the database. If there is a match, the user is cleared to pass.

Hand geometry readers are a good way to manage access control, with similar advantages to fingerprint readers. The primary disadvantages of hand geometry are its failure to recognize aging or injured hands. Also, by contrast, fingerprint scanners typically cost less and check users faster.

Facial recognition

Facial recognition evaluates the features of an individual's face, taking advantage of the fact that peoples' facial characteristics do not change much with aging. The faces are scanned from a distance of about two to three feet, where the complete facial structure can be measured, including distance between the eyes, nose, mouth, jaw, and edges. If a match to the scan is found within the system's database, access is granted.

Facial recognition is advantageous, due to its ease of integration into an existing access control mechanism and its quick identification time. On the other hand, facial recognition also has difficulty with changes in lighting conditions, background objects, variation in face positioning, and, sometimes, user facial changes such as expressions or hairstyles. More importantly, the possibility of using fake faces, created with masks or facial prosthetics, to pass through should be considered.

Facial recognition has an unpredictable future because of the variety of scenarios that can cause false positives or negatives in the recognition process when it is the only access control mechanism.

Iris scanning

The *iris* is the colored tissue around the eye's pupil. Iris scans evaluate parameters including, but not limited to, rings, furrows, and freckles of the eye. An iris scanning device measures these parameters from a distance of about two to three inches. Approximately two hundred points, based on specific parameters, are checked against an already stored database for a match. A match confirms the user is legitimate.

Because each person's iris is unique, iris scanning, if done precisely, is a very accurate method of identification and authorization. Again, while there is no requirement for users to remember passwords or carry ID cards, *two-step authentication* can combine iris scanning with a PIN, password, entry code, or other extra security.

An added advantage of iris scanning is that it cannot be fooled by a fake eye; a fake eye can be distinguished due to the lack of pupil dilation and absence of light reflection from inside the eye.

Iris scanning challenges include its high initial cost, potential difficulty for users to bring and hold their eye in front of an iris scanner, and incorrect readings. Incorrect readings can occur due to incorrect posture, poor lighting, and, possibly, an obscured iris due to drooping eyelids.

Retinal scanning

Scanning the *retina*, the light-sensitive membrane forming the inner lining of the back wall of the eyeball, is as accurate as iris scanning technology because it cannot be duplicated by a fake user. Retinal scanning uses a low-intensity light source and an optical coupler to read the retina patterns in the eye. Users look into a small hole, toward a light source, while keeping their heads still and eyesight focused onto the light for a few seconds. Retina scanning devices take around ten to fifteen seconds to pass or reject the user's identity.

The precision and accuracy of retina scanning is its most important advantage, and the high startup cost is its main disadvantage. Additionally, the invasive screening process may cause discomfort for some users, as they are required to remove glasses, bring their heads close to the device, and focus on the light for several seconds.

Vascular patterns

Vascular pattern recognition examines the unique thickness and arrangement of the network of veins in an individual's hand or, less often, face. Users place a hand on the elliptical surface of a vascular reader. The vascular reader scans the veins in the hand using infrared radiation. The output of this infrared scan is a picture that can either be stored in the database for the enrollment phase or matched with the existing pattern in the database for the recognition phase.

While vascular pattern recognition is a highly effective technology, its primary disadvantages, when compared with other biometric access control methods, are that more space is required for the vascular reader, injured hands may impede the verification process, and medical problems may affect the arrangement of veins and arteries.

Behavioral Biometric Techniques

While the previous biometric techniques dealt with static properties, other biometric techniques examine behavioral properties of human beings for unique identification. Common behavioral techniques include speech recognition, signature recognition, and keystroke recognition.

Speech recognition

Speech recognition systems maintain a database of authorized users' recorded voices. A user requesting entry is supposed to speak a pre-allocated passphrase into a microphone installed as part of the speech recognition system. The system then compares the user's voice with the database, and, if the match is successful, the user is granted entry.

Speech recognition system variations include:

- *Fixed phrase verification*: Users are given a fixed phrase for identification every time they need to use the system.
- *Fixed vocabulary verification*: In this case, instead of having pre-recorded a fixed phrase, a limited vocabulary check is often made, like PIN codes.

- *Flexible vocabulary verification*: This is an intelligent variation of the earlier versions where prompted strings of words are used as passphrases, thereby adding flexibility.

One of the major advantages of speech recognition access control systems is their low startup costs compared with several of the static biometric property access control systems. Speech recognition tools are also flexible, fast, accurate, and easily deployable, due to their inherent simplicity.

Signature recognition

In *signature recognition systems*, all authorized users submit their signatures as part of the enrollment process. The papers with the signatures are scanned and converted into digital records stores with the user's identity in a database. Later, in the recognition phase, users seeking access are asked to sign on the sensor, and the provided signature is digitized and then compared against the database. If a match is found, then the user is granted access.

The latest signature recognition technologies examine parameters like writing speed, directions, and pressures of writing as well as contact angle and points of the writing stylus.

Like speech recognition systems, signature recognition systems are also low-cost and easily deployable. They also provide significant accuracy and precision in the verification process.

Keystroke recognition

In *keyboard recognition systems*, users' passwords and parameters related to their typing style are stored with the system's database. Every time users try to log on to the system with their passwords, the related parameters are also checked to identify them.

The parameters can include the pressure on the keys while typing; time taken to type certain specific words; time elapsed between pressing the keys; and finger placement on the keys while typing, including variances for left and right hands.

The obvious advantage of keystroke recognition systems is that they are purely computer-based; there are no special requirements, and no enrollment phase is needed to begin building the database. Instead, the database is filled by collecting users' keystroke parameters while they are making normal use of the system.

Another big advantage of a keystroke recognition system is that it is totally software-based. Unlike the other biometric systems, there is no hardware cost. The only hardware needed is already part of the system—the keyboard.

However, the downside is that keyboard stroke recognition is not widely accepted, due to the variety of normal scenarios that can cause false negatives and false positives. The software needs improvement to accurately and more precisely capture users' keystroke habits.

Security Issues with Biometric Access Control Technologies

Like all other security measures, biometric technology is not foolproof. Access control and authorization breaches should still be considered after installing biometric access control devices. Some common security issues with biometric technology are:

- **Fraudulent enrollment:** Fraud in the enrollment phase, either intentionally by attackers or unintentionally by authorized users, may lead to incorrect data in the database, which can eventually be used by unauthorized users to gain access.

- *Multiple enrollments*: These are possible if the system operators and administrators are not using proper procedures in the enrollment process.
- *Enrolling a difficult image*: Sometimes users unintentionally enroll an image, such as a tilted head or a squashed finger, which is later difficult to match. This leads to false negatives when the system is unable to verify the legitimate user, reducing the system's integrity.
- *Invalid data*: Invalid data, either due to unintentional mistakes by authorized users or malicious intent by an attacker, will lead to false verifications.
- *Confusing data*: Sometimes, a person with an injury or physical disability may confuse the system. The technology is not prepared for all scenarios.
- *Lookalikes*: Similar to confusing data, two or more biometric signatures may end up too much alike. This is rare, due to the generally unique properties measured by biometric systems, but the problem of lookalikes is more likely to occur when the biometric scans are less detailed than necessary.

- **Fatigued operator:** Some biometric systems leave difficult matching decisions to the human mind. However, a fatigued operator could make a mistake, leading to a security breach.
- **Identity only, without security:** Biometric systems provide only identity verification; they are not used to unlock a mechanism that is actually providing security, such as a locked door or gate.
- **Dependence on other systems:** Biometric scanners are always attached to a system that grants access based on the result of data matching provided by biometric scanner. That means the biometric scanners will always communicate the result (true or false) of a data match to the access control system, such as a mechanism for opening a door. This communication,

if forged by a MITM attack, for example, can render the biometric scanning useless.[56]

- **Aging changes biometric properties:** Some biometric technologies fail to detect changes due to users' aging.
- **Regeneration of biometric images from templates is possible:** Last, but not least, attackers can employ algorithms to regenerate legitimate biometric images from other image templates. Though it is a time-consuming method, it is also effective and poses a potential threat to biometric technologies used today.

---

[56] Refer to Chapter 8 for more discussion about MITM attacks.

CHAPTER

Social Engineering

With all of the different security precautions available today—system and network hardening, installing antivirus software, establishing VPNs, putting in physical security mechanisms, etc.—attackers often choose a simpler method. Instead of breaking all of the security perimeters, the attacker focuses on persuading insiders to make mistakes that lead to a security breach. These types of attacks are generally referred to as *social engineering*.

What is Social Engineering?

Social engineering attacks benefit from faulty human decision-making skills by convincing the target user to act against proper security policies. For example, an employee gets an email from an unknown sender with a subject line "Mass Company Downsizing," then downloads and opens an attachment secretly hiding a virus, worm, or Trojan horse. Proper security policy would say to never open an email attachment from an unknown sender, but, in this case, an attractive subject line convinced the employee to violate this policy.

Although information and computer security technologies provide safeguards, all of the latest security technology is futile when the attacker uses social engineering to exploit flawed human judgment. Here's another potential scenario:

> An attacker calls an Internet service provider (ISP) to reset his email password, pretending to be the manager of the company. He makes up a story that he has forgotten the password and needs to send a very important, time-sensitive email, or the company's possibility of winning a contract could be jeopardized. The person working for the ISP feels pressured because of the apparent authority of the executive and the importance of the task that needs to be done, so he resets the password and provides it to the attacker. The attacker can then use the manager's email account to send unsolicited emails, get a hold of confidential emails, and wreak havoc within the company. Here, a subtle and soft attack has defeated all of the company's good practices and investments in security.

Many times, attackers and criminals use social engineering by manipulating human psychology, rather than by breaching or utilizing hacking techniques. Instead of trying to find a software vulnerability to breach, a social engineer may just call an employee, pretend to be an IT support person, and trick the employee into disclosing his or her passwords and other personal information.

Social engineering is not a new invention; the strategy has been used for ages, sometimes in legitimate ways. For example, when a child does not feel like going to school and refuses to go, her parents might try to persuade her using social engineering techniques instead of forcing her. Advertisements are mostly based on social engineering techniques to convince shoppers to buy a product or service they otherwise would not have thought of buying. In these examples, the subject or target takes some kind of action that he or she would not have taken without persuasion from the other party.

Social engineering—What is the risk?

Social engineering is a proven method of breaking into an otherwise secure system. An attacker with a system password can log on, look around, and make changes to the system for as long as desired. The attacker may find a repository of sensitive data or gain access privileges to a physical facility, depending on the type of privileges attached to the compromised password.

Social engineering makes it easier to break into the physical security perimeter when more human beings are involved in physical security mechanisms. For example:

- If an employee who has come to the office without a photo ID can be allowed entry after a bit of scrutiny by a human guard or other employee, an attacker just needs a small team, perhaps including a rogue employee, to gain access by utilizing social engineering techniques, such as pretending to be in an urgent rush.
- Lost ID cards, keys, or passwords are usually dealt with in a way convenient for legitimate users, such as over the phone. Attackers can use social engineering techniques, take advantage of these processes, and request duplicate cards or reset the password of a legitimate employee to gain the legitimate employee's access.
- Any time non-employees are allowed access to typically secure areas of the premises, such as when procedures allow personnel bring in new equipment or make repairs, there is a potential for social engineering attacks.
- Mechanisms for deploying new builds, installing patches, and version upgrades are also prone to social engineering attacks by disgruntled employees or outsiders delegated with such tasks.
- Mechanisms for responding to customer queries and complaints can reveal classified information to an attacker who is pretending to be furious or may be too curious.
- General or standing order procedures for handling law enforcement agencies, taxation staff, or auditors are also weak links that can be used in a social engineering attack. The attacker may pretend to be an employee of a trusted organization and request access to the system.

The most efficient way to identify social engineering risks is by concentrating on security procedures handled by human beings. No automated system can be convinced or pressured to reset a password. Systems can only be breached; humans can be socially engineered. After identifying the human-controlled areas of a security system, build on these scenarios and test them to both evaluate and train the security staff. The best defense against social engineering is helping people understand the threat.

Typical Social Engineering Attack Types on IT Systems

Spam

Spam—unwanted email, usually by commercial companies—is a nuisance for all email users. Individuals are bombarded with spam on a daily basis, although most, but not all, spam is often blocked by using *spam filters*. Without spam filters, using email would be a terrible experience for the users.

Other than being annoying, spam is extensively used for social engineering. Spam emails are often used to market deceitful or dangerous products. Additionally, spam is commonly used to distribute Trojan horses, worms, viruses, and other malware products.

The load on a network due to spam transmission and storage is quite significant. Often, spam uses images, rather than mere text, in order to appear larger and avoid detection from spam filters and detection programs.

Phishing

Phishing attacks are the online equivalent to someone calling claiming to be from your bank asking for your credit card details. Typically, a user receives an email that appears to have come from a trustworthy sender or business associate. The message takes the user to what appears to be an authentic web page, where the user is likely fooled into leaking critical information to the attacker. Many individuals have fallen victim to phishing. Guidelines for avoiding such attacks include:

- Do not open emails from unknown senders.
- Do not follow links in emails unless you are the intended recipient of that email.
- Make sure the URL of any link in the email is a legitimate site by hovering the mouse over the link to ensure that the full URL of the destination matches the link description.
- Be cautious and note any modified URLs in the links within the email.
- Do not open unexpected attachments.
- Never give out passwords. No administrators should require the password of a user.
- Whenever a suspected phishing email or a website is encountered, report it to the network administrator as soon as possible.

Spear phishing

As discussed above, normal phishing attacks are not directed to any particular person; rather, they are generic in nature, looking for any victim. They tend to affect as many victims as possible. By contrast, *spear phishing* attacks are targeted at particular users by pretending to be someone they trust to get their personal information. For example, an attacker, alleging to be from PayPal, might send an email to a PayPal user asking him to change his password due to some security concern. However, the link to the PayPal site may be a phishing PayPal site address; it is a fake address only designed to capture the changed password of that particular user. Another example would be an attacker aiming to get a company's senior executive to download a worm. In that case, the attacker might formulate a phishing email specifically for that particular executive, such as crafting the message to add certain specific details related to the executive. These specific details would encourage the executive to respond positively and be more likely to believe that the message has come from a trusted source.

Hoaxes

Hoaxes are messages made to look real but are actually fabricated to deceive or trick people, such as reporting a fake bomb threat to a law enforcement agency. In many cases, hoaxes are sent as a joke. Still, they may be harmful and a source of embarrassment to the people believing and sharing them. Sometimes, targeted hoaxes are employed against a victim to damage the victim's own system through an improper action. For example, an attacker may generate and send to a naïve user a hoax message convincing the user to delete a specific file because it is malware from the Internet, when, in truth, the file is a harmless, but important, system file.

Pretexting

In this type of social engineering attack, a superficial scenario, known as the *pretext*, is crafted to engage a specific victim in a way that increases the chances of that victim falling prey to it and revealing personal or organizational information or acting in a way that would not be possible otherwise. Pretext is a decorative lie involving some earlier research or arrangement and usage of data for imitation (e.g., Social Security number, date of birth, etc.) to convince the target that the attacker is a legitimate source.

Pretexting has been used by business rivals to try fooling each other into divulging client data; by investigators to get telephone, utility, and banking archives, and other such information from company employees; and by impersonators to masquerade as colleagues, police, banking or tax authorities, insurance detectives, or some other authoritative individual. Attackers using pretexting are typically well-prepared for the questions a victim might ask. In most cases, it is the attacker's confidence that ultimately allows them to deceive the victim.

Baiting

In social engineering attacks involving *baiting*, attackers lure in victims to persuade them to do what the attacker wants. The main idea behind baiting is tempting the victim with the expectation of some entertainment, benefit, reward, or gain. For example, a music or movie download from a peer-to-peer site may include a hidden host of malware. Similarly, a USB pen drive marked with an organization's logo and the title "Salary Raise Plan—2016" placed out in the open for employees of the organization to find could secretly include malware to give an attacker access to secured information.

Quid pro quo

Quid pro quo means a bargain where one gets something in exchange for something else. When quid pro quo is employed in social engineering attacks, the impression of a bargain is implanted in the mind of victim, even though nothing is said explicitly.

For example, an administrator may be stuck on an important technical issue. A social engineering attacker may offer to resolve the administrator's problem, and then, once the administrator has accepted, the attacker will ask the administrator to provide access to a resource for which the attacker is not authorized. Though no such deal was made between them beforehand, the administrator might feel a moral obligation to comply with the attacker's demand.

Another case might be an attacker pretending to be from some fictitious organization and roaming a crowded shopping mall giving out free pens or USB flash drives or some other small items for free in exchange for people filling out information forms with some of their personal credentials.

Tailgating/Piggybacking

In *tailgating* or *piggybacking*, attackers seeking access to a restricted zone guarded only by automated systems without human guards gain entry behind an authorized person with legitimate access privilege.

Tailgating is typically a crude case of social engineering employed by attackers abusing extended social courtesies. A common example of this kind of attack is the courtesy of an individual with legitimate access holding a door open for another, at their request, who is not authorized to enter the building. People like the legitimate user do not ask for identification, or may simply be complacent. The attacker may indicate forgotten verification or may even produce a fake token (such as an ID card) just to show it to the legitimate user but not to use at the automated access control station.

Another variant of tailgating can be when an attacker asks for a mobile phone or laptop from a victim for just a moment to check his email or make a phone call because he forgot his own device. However, in the process, the attacker installs something malicious, accesses a malicious website, or opens malware in the email, thereby infecting the victim's device.

Countermeasures to Social Engineering Attacks

Social engineering attacks can be devastating and can happen even with good security measures in place. Organizations and individuals can adopt various countermeasures to reduce the chances of successful of social engineering attacks against them. These countermeasures are described below.

- **Establish an environment of trust at the employee level.** All employees must know what information or data is sensitive and must be protected at all costs, whether they can access it themselves or not.
- **Create threat scenarios based on social engineering techniques.** Use these scenarios to train employees and prepare them for these types of attacks. This way, employees who are actually the target of an attack can educate themselves on how to handle the situation.
- **Put security policies and procedures in place for handling sensitive information.** These policies and procedures should be frequently reviewed.
- **Train each and every person in the organization in relevant security protocols.** The employees must be periodically briefed on social engineering attacks, alongside other security education.
- **Security administrators must periodically do unannounced testing.** This can be achieved by pretending to be an attacker and performing social engineering attacks to see how employees respond. Accordingly, employees may need to be retrained.
- **Concentrate on mechanisms wholly or partially managed by human beings.**

Steps in a Typical Social Engineering Attack

Typically, a social engineering attack is implemented using the following steps:

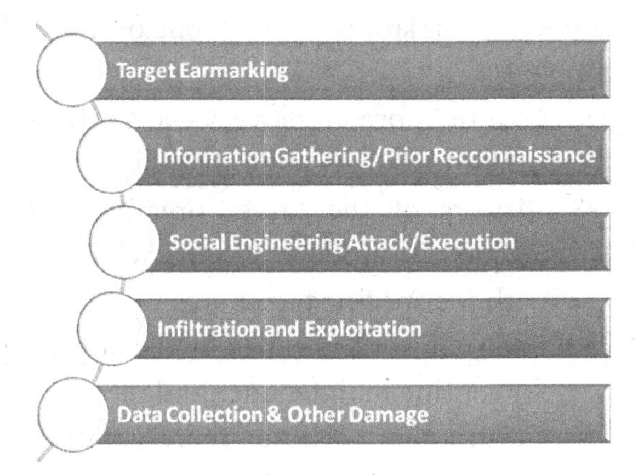

Figure: 15.1: Steps in social engineering

- **Target earmarking:** In many cases, a target has already been chosen by the attacker. The target may be a specific victim, or the attacker might target a general area of interest, such as a type of business.
- **Information gathering:** The attacker, like conventional criminals, gathers lots of information about their target through means such as:
  - An organization's website may give sufficient information about the organization's products and service, goals, and employee numbers.
  - An organization's customer relations office or help desk can be contacted for further details. Some social engineering skills may be required by the attacker so as not to reveal the plan.
  - Packet sniffers employed intelligently around the perimeters of a network may reveal further information,

like network IP addresses, network devices, number of hosts, type of services, and even the number of servers.
    - An attacker may carry out a physical survey, especially if the attacker is planning a physical security breach.
    - Before the social engineering attack, the attacker may try to develop a relationship with one or more of following people:
        - One or more employees—a frustrated employee can be especially helpful to the attacker
        - Visitors of the target organization, especially frequent visitors or visitors who have a concern with the specific target area
        - External workers called by the target organization for routine maintenance and repair
        - Contractors, whose representatives visit the organization on a regular basis
        - Security staff

- **Social engineering attack/execution:** After acquiring the necessary information about the target, the attacker starts making plans for a social engineering attack. This phase usually lasts until the attacker is successful in the social engineering attack. Once successful, the attacker may be able to install malware, like backdoor or a Trojan horse, into the organization's system. With the passage of time and number of tries, depending upon the attacker's skills and the organization's preventative measures, the attacker may also get more information to launch further attacks.
- **Infiltration and exploitation:** The attacker capitalizes on the gains of the social attack. Armed with specific information and confidential data about entry into the system, the attacker will now act to infiltrate and further exploit his achievements. The attacker may proceed in the following manner, depending upon the type of information attained or damage done earlier with social engineering:

- Utilize installed backdoors to install further malware onto the systems
- Access confidential information, with the help of a Trojan horse, from the data storage of the organization under attack
- Carry out a DoS single system or botnet attack after having obtained sufficient information about the organization's network devices[57]
- Use malware to forge emails
- Use malware to modify or delete data, thereby compromising the data integrity

- **Data collection or other damage:** Attackers successful in the previous phases may choose to gather more data and cause other types of damage, such as stealing customer credentials or conducting fraudulent credit card activities. In rare cases, the attacker may try to get out without leaving any forensic evidence.

[57] Refer to Chapter 8 for a discussion about DoS and botnet attacks in greater depth.

CHAPTER

Mobile Security

Trends in Mobile Security

As important as security technologies are for safeguarding computer systems, networks, applications, and data, mobile security issues and technology are also a growing concern.

Today's *mobile devices* include tablets, smart phones, and other handheld devices using an operating system and similar functionality and architecture. These devices have become top-priority gadgets in today's environment—fulfilling multiple needs related to communication, entertainment, socialization, traveling, net-surfing, etc. In short, modern life without a mobile device is difficult.

Enhancement of mobile device hardware and software occurs rapidly. Unfortunately, security features are not improving nearly as quickly. Therefore, mobile devices, due to their extensive usage and comparatively less elaborate security features, have become a lucrative playground for malicious parties. Many organizations consider mobile phone usage at the workplace a threat to their security.

Main Challenges to Mobile Security

Inherent security challenges faced by mobile device users include:

- *Data storage risks*: Data loss can happen when a user loses a mobile device or when an attacker uses a malicious application. Data stored in the mobile device can include personal information like name, address, date of birth, financial information, family photos, social networking details, and emails. In addition, work information may be available on the phone, including employee details, work position, contact numbers, and possibly official documents.
- *Physical security*: Physical security of a mobile device is a greater challenge than security of computers, laptops, and other larger gadgets. The portability of mobile devices makes them more prone to theft or loss.
- *Internet browsing*: While mobile devices are extensively used for Internet surfing, this activity reveals quite a few vulnerabilities. For example, because a mobile user normally cannot see the full web address, it can be difficult to know whether a site is safe, especially in relation to phishing attacks. Mobile browsing also leaves users open to injection threats, including SQL injection, cross site scripting, and text-based attacks. [58]
- *Multiple user logging*: Many mobile device applications promote the use of a single sign-on, such as using a social media account to log on to a third-party application. But this means that attackers who crack a user's social media password may gain access to all applications using the same credentials, providing the attacker with additional information pertaining to the user.
- *Session handling*: Improper session handling creates lots of vulnerabilities for mobile devices while Internet surfing or

[58] Refer to Chapter 4 for discussion of injection threats in greater depth.

using applications. Sessions with extended expiration times invite vulnerabilities, especially while performing financial tasks. Incorrect session management may lead to illegal access through session hijacking. For example, an attacker can steal a user's authentication cookies for a particular session and use them to access the user's account.

- *Weak authentication issues*: Most mobile applications depend upon password authentication only. Not enforcing strong passwords and insecurity of valuable credentials by the mobile application developers expose mobile users to a number of threats, such as stolen credentials and automated brute force attacks.

Threats and Vulnerabilities Related to Mobile Devices

Noteworthy threats and vulnerabilities related to today's mobile devices, commonly resulting in compromised data, include:

- **Physical threats**
  - *Bluetooth*: *Bluetooth* is a very short range communication mechanism relied upon for sharing small files among mobile users. However, this means it can spread malware as well.
  - *Lost or stolen mobile devices*: Loss of a mobile device means loss of all personal credentials and data stored on the mobile device.

- **Application-based threats**
  - *Spyware*: They collect personal data, usage statistics, and interests of the user for bombardment of ads through adware.[59]

[59] Refer to Chapter 5 for an exploration of spyware and adware in greater detail.

- *Malware*: Malware have been created to target each and every mobile operating system.[60]
- *Vulnerable applications*: Mobile applications are developed for all operating systems on daily basis. Many of them are even available for free. However, these mobile applications often include both intentional and unintentional vulnerabilities, which are a constant threat to the user.
- *Privacy threats*: By gaining access to data stored on a mobile device, an attacker can capture user location data, steal a user's identity, and learn user activities and interests.

- **Network-based threats**
  - *Denial of service attacks (DoS)*: DoS attacks can also affect mobile services.[61]
  - *Network exploits*: Mobile devices are vulnerable to any exploits in the wireless network used by the device for Internet use or for communication. This vulnerability extends to additional services used by mobile devices including:
    - *SMS*: *Short Messaging Service* exchanges text messages between mobile phones through the mobile service provider's messaging server.
    - *MMS*: *Multimedia Messaging Service* exchanges text, picture, and video between mobile phones, utilizing mobile networks.
    - *VoIP*: *Voice over Internet Protocol* is a service used to make multimedia calls over data networks, such as the Internet.

---

[60] Refer to Chapter 5 for more about malware.

[61] Refer to Chapter 8 for a description of DoS attacks in greater detail.

- *Wi-Fi sniffing*: *Wi-Fi sniffing* is the interception of data between a mobile device and wireless access points. Unencrypted data is especially vulnerable to this action.

- **Web-based threats**
    - *Drive-by downloads*: Some malicious applications are designed to be automatically downloaded to a user's mobile device when the user visits a particular website.[62]
    - *Browser exploits*: These types of attacks exploit the browser vulnerabilities of mobile devices.
    - *Phishing scams*: Mobile devices are vulnerable to phishing attacks, including through SMS/MMS.[63]

- **Malware threats**[64]
    - *Rootkit*: They can infect a mobile device's operating system files and hide underneath.
    - *Worm*: Traditional worms can threaten a mobile device's operating system and applications. The interconnected mobile environment allows worms to spread rapidly.
    - *Trojan horse*: Trojan horses in the mobile ecosystem are employed for stealing information, phishing attacks, and spreading worms.
    - *Botnet*: Traditional botnets may include mobile devices as well.

Popular mobile device defensive mechanisms

Compared with typical computer systems, mobile devices have more vulnerabilities and, therefore, more threats to the user data, due to peculiarities regarding the mobile platform and user patterns. Though the countermeasures against such threats are not catching

[62] Refer to Chapter 5 for more on drive-by downloads.

[63] Refer to Chapter 15 for more about phishing.

[64] Refer to Chapter 5 for greater discussion about each of these malware threats.

up as fast, many defensive mechanisms may be adopted by various stakeholders, including:

- *Application stores and developers*: Most, if not all, mobile device operating systems have their own application stores. Android, iOS, Windows, and Blackberry have their own application stores with guidelines for developers. Despite this scrutiny, the mobile ecosystem has no lack of malware and data-stealing applications. Generally, operating system vendors have spent more time keeping the market growing by offering new applications to users and not enough time scrutinizing submitted applications.
- *Application permissions*: While installing any application, the user has to explicitly grant the requested permissions for that application. Operating systems even provide users with the option to see the permissions granted to an application later. However, in many cases, the permissions list can be unclear and hard for users to understand.
- *Operating system security features*: Mobile operating systems have a host of security features in their core and API frameworks to handle the fragile security environment in today's competitive world.[65] Detailed information on such security features offered by mobile operating systems is available for developers, users, or anybody to read, evaluate, and utilize. However, most of a mobile operating system's security features are incapacitated when the device is *jail broken* by removing the vendor's restrictions from the device. Moreover, few mobile users use most operating system security features properly or correctly.

---

[65] *Application Programming Interface (API) framework* is provided by the operating system so that third-party application developers can use an operating system's features and hardware resources.

- *Hardware security*: Popular mobile device hardware security features include biometrics and secure packaging, such as cases and other protectors.
- *Third-party security applications*: Mobile-specific antivirus programs have been developed to guard against malware like viruses, worms, rootkit, spyware, and adware. Proper use of updated antivirus tools can build a reasonable defense against malware.
- *Best practices*: Apart from default security features in the operating system and device, users can take several precautionary measures to guard against security threats, including:
    - Shunning complacency by giving due weight to security
    - Maintaining secure custody of the device and password
    - Correctly configuring operating system features like permissions, use of resources, and access to data by applications
    - Installing applications only from trusted sources
    - Using updated antivirus programs and applications
    - Observing the behavior of applications
    - Being cautious of the permissions being utilized by applications
    - Abiding by safe browsing and emailing tips
    - Encrypting sensitive data or not keeping sensitive data on a mobile device at all
    - Actively listening for security-related news

Mobile Device Management (MDM) Solutions

Mobile device management solutions (*MDM*) are employed by organizations to manage and administer mobile device usage on their premises. While some see the inherent threats and vulnerabilities related to mobile device usage as organizational security threats, others recognize the utility of mobile devices for both personal and organizational use. Therefore, the current trend is for organizations to deploy a centralized MDM solution and register all employees' mobile devices. That allows security staff to better manage and administer control of mobile device usage and applications and access of devices to organizational resources.

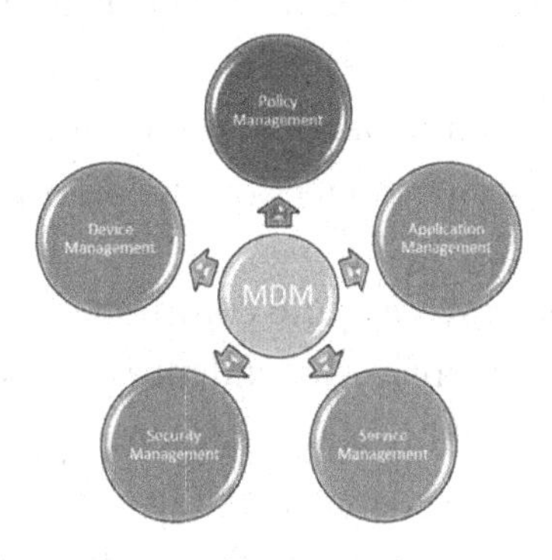

Figure 16.1: Mobile device management solution

Approaches to MDM

MDM can be obtained from a mobile service provider to manage mobile devices utilizing that particular provider's services. Using this type of MDM would require the organization to restrict employees' use of mobile services to that particular service provider.

Another approach is a third-party solution, where all mobile devices utilizing various mobile service providers' services could be managed through one platform. While this approach would need a lot of customization, it would be cost-effective.

Another debate is whether to allow employees to bring their personal mobile devices (BYOD – bring your own device) to the enterprise premises at all. The solution to this issue varies from organization to organization. Because mobile devices are so widely used for so many purposes, it is recommended to allow employees to BYOD. However, a system relying on BYOD should be managed by centralized MDM to safeguard organizational resources.

Threats to organizations from mobile devices

Two scenarios assess the threat mobile devices can present to an organization. The first scenario is one where the organization does not depend on mobile devices. This is quite rare nowadays, as employees often need to be reached away from the office. However, if the organization is not dependent on mobile devices, it can simply prohibit the use of mobile devices on the premises.

The other scenario, which is quite common, is that the organization has either limited or extensive dependence on mobile device usage for routine work. Then, the threat arises when employees' mobile devices are storing organizational data, using the organization's applications, utilizing the organization's network and Internet services, and, in some cases, keeping location services on while on the organization's premises. Other careless actions include taking photos of critical areas and organization resources, talking casually about company classified information, and casual use of SMS/MMS services. The danger of these possibilities forces organizations to take security safeguards to protect their interests.

Features of centralized MDM for enterprise

Today's organizations must consider the multiple security features of a centralized MDM solution in order to properly manage and control employees' mobile device usage on the premises. First and foremost, the centralized MDM solution should be able to implement the organization's general security policy. The following points are additional suggestions, which may or may not be applicable to a particular organization, depending on its security policy:

- Restrict the use of mobile device peripherals, such as cameras, GPS, and Bluetooth.
- Restrict native operating system services, such as browsing and email.

- Manage Wi-Fi connectivity.
- Restrict any discrepancies between configuration and allowed settings.
- Limit or prevent access to organizational resources.
- Encrypt data communication between the organization and mobile devices.
- Encrypt internal and external storage data.
- Reset or reformat the mobile device to its default settings before issuing it to an employee.
- Format the device remotely, in case of its loss.
- Control incorrect authentication attempts.
- Restrict application stores or enforce whitelisting/blacklisting of applications.[66]
- Restrict synchronizing services that move data to cloud servers.
- Enforce digital certificates.
- Manage applications, updates, and patches remotely.

Deploying centralized MDM solutions and customizing them according to the security needs of the organization is a growing trend focused on keeping employees productive and guarding the organization's resources.

---

[66] Refer to Chapter 6 for more information about whitelisting and blacklisting.

CHAPTER

Current Trends in Information Security

Information security professionals and attackers have been battling one another throughout the evolution of information technology (IT). Almost all technologies created to safeguard against attacks have their own weaknesses and vulnerabilities. But this is not because the technologies are flawed in the first place; rather, security professionals make safeguards, and then attackers find the exploits. There is no end to it.

Defenders and security professionals have always had the advantage of choosing the security options, including design, secure software coding, placement of protection devices, and installation of antivirus software. However, the defenders have also faced a great disadvantage: most users are not aware of the necessary security measures, and, thus, problems arise as a result of human error, rather than the technology itself.

The attacker's main advantage is the ability to pick and choose the battlefield—where and when the attack will happen. The attacker could be an expert, in some cases with more knowledge than the security team. By contrast, the victim is typically a normal user, with no extensive knowledge of the system. Because the tug-of-war between security professionals and attackers is a constant struggle in IT, it is imperative for users not to get complacent with information security procedures. Users should stay informed about both the latest information security technologies and the latest attacks. Often, the most protected users are the ones who invest in enhanced security, keep an eye on security news, and acquaint themselves with the latest attacks, technologies, and mechanisms for better safeguards.

This chapter provides an overview of the current trends in information security—the techniques and technologies widely adopted over the last few years. This does not include ideas still in inception and yet to be embraced by the market.

Unified Threat Management (UTM)

Unified threat management (*UTM*), also known as *unified security management* (*USM*), did not gain a lot of popularity when it was first introduced, but it is now an established primary network security solution.

UTM proposes unifying multiple information and computer security products into a single system. These products include traditional firewalls, intrusion detection systems, intrusion prevention systems, and antivirus or anti-spam software. Moreover, UTM aims at combining functions like content filtering, VPN tunneling, data loss prevention, and load balancing as part of the same UTM interface.

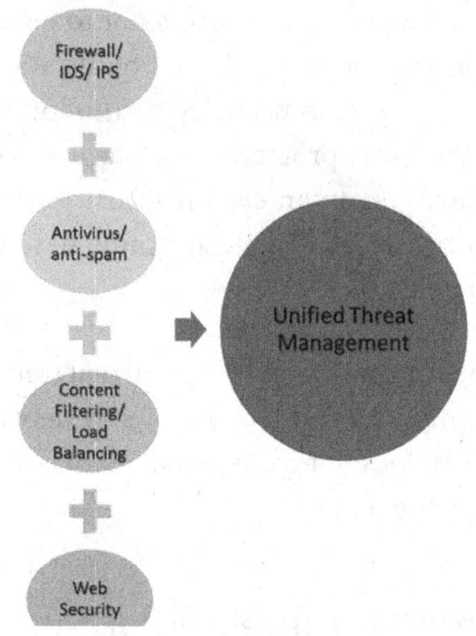

Figure 17.1: Unified threat management

Individual threat management vs. integrated management

UTM avoids the need to separately oversee multiple individual security products. Managing too many security devices can not only be cumbersome, it can also increase operational complexities and costs by presenting issues such as conflict resolution, false sense of security, difficulty of similar configuration setup, challenges in imposing policies, and burdensome monitoring. On the other hand, a solitary UTM machine can combine all security functionality into one rack-mounted device. The main benefits of deploying a UTM solution are its simplicity, efficient installation and usage, and ability to manage and configure all security utilities simultaneously. Therefore, today's organizations prefer an integrated network security solution that combines the management and administration of various devices.

Pros and cons of UTM devices as compared to traditional security

- *Pros.* A UTM solution provides the following advantages:
  - Managerial security is simplified.
  - Monitoring and configuring of all security solutions at once is attractive.
  - A UTM device's customized operating system provides ease of monitoring and configuration management, an interactive web interface with minimal configuration settings, no requirement for multiple application installations, and easy updating with patches and version control.
  - Minimal technical training is required for a UTM system when compared to the technical training needed for multiple security devices with different expertise and experience requirements.
  - For organizations with several site offices and remote networks, UTM provides a central security control on all distributed networks around the globe.
  - Lower long-term costs are expected with UTM solutions than managing multiple devices, even though UTM requires a greater initial investment for acquisition and installation.

- *Cons.* Like every other technology, UTM solutions also come with a few drawbacks.
  - Being the single security boss means any fault in the UTM system would result in chaos. Therefore, redundancy and high availability for UTM systems cannot be overemphasized.
  - Similar to the point above, as the UTM device is a single point of failure, its compromise or inability to guard against an attack presents an easy opening for repeated attacks.

- A UTM system always requires enormous computing power, memory, and other resources. A shortage of available resources would affect latency and bandwidth, thereby leading to poor performance.

Security Information and Event Management (SIEM)

Security information and event management (*SIEM*) is a combination of *security information management* (*SIM*)—providing lasting storage as well as investigation and recording data logs— and *security event management* (*SEM*)—dealing with online monitoring and association of events, reports, and views.

SIEM systems provide all-inclusive observation of an organization's information security. The fundamental principle of a SIEM system is that observing and monitoring network data and security from a single location makes it easier to spot tendencies and suspect designs.

SIEM systems are sold as both software products and services and are useful for generating security logs and reports for compliance purposes. The key benefit of SIEM comes from real-time analysis of security warnings generated by network hardware and software.

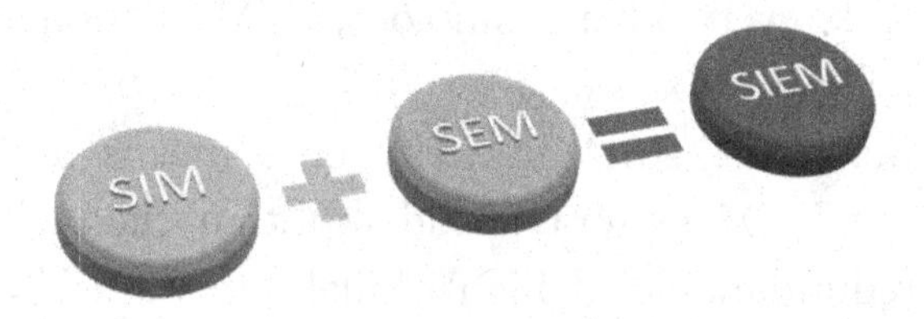

Figure 17.2: Security information and event management system

How are SIEM systems deployed?

A SIEM system is expected to gather logs and other security-related documents for scrutiny. For a SIEM system to work, its agents must be deployed hierarchically to collect security-related happenings from end-user devices, network devices, servers, and security equipment such as firewalls, antivirus software, and intrusion detection/prevention systems. The agents pass on events to a central management console, which reviews and flags irregularities. For the SIEM system to correctly identify malicious activities, the administrators must first enter the typical profile of the system under normal conditions.

Typical methodology of SIEM systems

A SIEM system monitors other security devices, such as firewalls, IDS/IPS, etc. These other security devices are referred to as the SIEM system's *edge collectors*. The workload of the SIEM solution can be reduced considerably if some sorting is done at the edge collectors and only processed information is passed onto SIEM system's central management module. In this manner, the amount of information is reduced. However, the drawback is that, in some cases, important events may be filtered out in pre-processing.

When the SIEM system has all of the necessary data regarding events and information, it carries out a central investigation of and reports on security incidents. This process is able to detect attacks that could not be detected by other means. On top of it, some SIEM systems have the capability to stop attacks that are in progress by communicating with other security devices, such as firewalls and IPS/IDS, and instructing them to alter their configurations to stop the malicious activity.[67]

---

[67] Refer to Chapter 9 for more about firewalls. Refer to Chapter 10 for more about IDS/IPS.

The expanding scope of SIEM

The concept of SIEM is not new. SIEM systems have been available for quite some time, but earlier SIEM systems were directed at large organizations with refined security capabilities and a substantial amount of security staff. More recent SIEM systems include installable software variants, for local hardware or virtual machines, and cloud variants, available through a private or public cloud, all of which can be well-suited to the needs of small and medium-sized organizations.

SIEM system usage profiles and accrued benefits

SIEM products are used for multiple purposes and offer a variety of benefits including:

- *Compliance reporting*: A lot of organizations just want the convenience of running their compliance reporting through a central log framework. All hosts or devices required to have their security events included in the SIEM reporting have to transfer their logs to a SIEM system. The benefit is that all sorts of logs of various kinds of hosts are combined into a single log produced by the SIEM server. It is created in one format, which makes it easier to understand. This also simplifies the reporting process in the hierarchy. However, organizations not already using SIEM systems are unlikely to have a strong central log competency that can produce the customizable reporting necessary for compliance. For those organizations, it is necessary to generate individual reports for all hosts or retrieve data from each host and then collect and reproduce it centrally for manual report generation, but this is very difficult for reasons including:
    - Dissimilar operating systems on various machines
    - Different log formats and reports for dissimilar devices and vendors

- Required extensive coding and customization to try to automate the process itself by converting of all the information to the same format.

- *Detection of incidents which may not otherwise be detected by individual efforts of multiple devices and mechanisms*: SIEM systems present a unified front against security threats. Individual devices may be very efficient, but their overall efficiency is similar to the strength of a chain—focused in its weakest link. A SIEM system, on the other hand, consolidates the security strengths and covers up the weaknesses. This allows a SIEM system to detect incidents that would be otherwise undetectable.

Many hosts do not have incident detection capabilities. They can monitor events and produce audit logs but lack the ability to analyze and identify malicious activities. But SIEM systems have the ability to fuse otherwise incomplete information from different sources about the same incident into one meaningful piece of information by collecting, collating, pre-processing, and then intelligently fusing the data. Fusing events from different sources allows a SIEM system to view attacks with bits and pieces seen by different sources and devices, and then reconstruct the series of events to determine the nature of the attack and whether it was successful. IDS and IPS, antivirus software, or firewalls may only come across a fraction of an attack, but the SIEM system can investigate the logs for all of these fractions of incidents, discover the nature of the attack, and raise alarms.

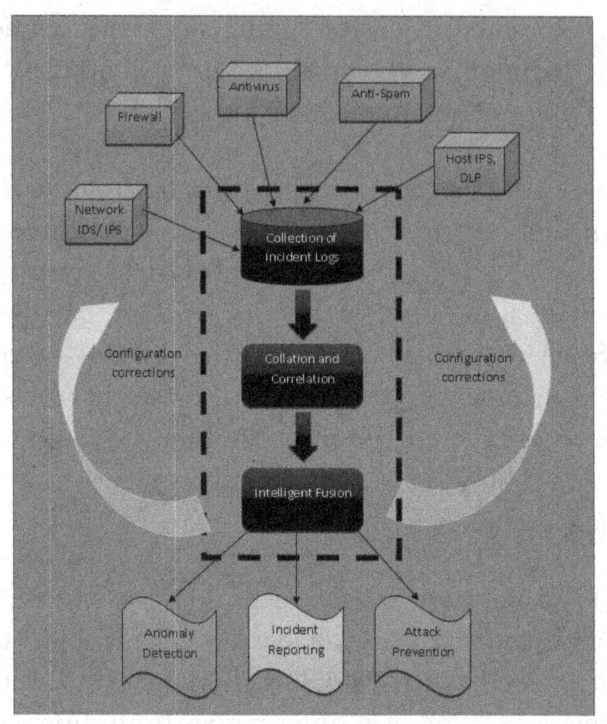

Figure 17.3: SIEM typical functionality

- *Utilizing traditional security devices.* SIEM systems do not replace traditional security devices; rather, they utilizes the work done by them. A lone SIEM system would be useless, due to its inability to monitor raw security events as they occur; a SIEM system requires processed information about security incidents from edge collectors to handle or safeguard against security incidents. Furthermore, a SIEM system can be configured to consume threat intelligence inputs from reliable external sources. The SIEM system will then terminate or otherwise upset recognized malicious hosts' connections with the organization's hosts in order to proactively prevent attacks.
- *Efficient incident handling.* Without a doubt, SIEM products meaningfully save time and assets for incident handlers. This in turn speeds up incident containment and reduces the amount of damage that a number of incidents may cause. Primarily, SIEM systems improve efficiency by using

a single interface to watch all of the security logs coming from multiple devices. A few instances where a SIEM system can accelerate incident handling include:

- Allowing an incident handler to swiftly detect an attack's path through the organization
- Facilitating swift detection of all hosts affected by a particular instance of malicious activity
- Containing and stopping attacks in progress, through preset mechanisms that are impossible without a SIEM system, due to the limited time duration of an attack when compared with the absence of an automated fusion mechanism.

Key differences between UTM and SIEM

It is important to recognize the differences between UTM and SIEM.

UTM is intended to actively manage the threat spectrum, combining the functionality of firewalls, VPNs, IDS/IPS, antivirus, and anti-spam into a single system. Therefore, if a UTM system is installed, the need for multiple separate security devices is automatically removed.

On the other hand, a SIEM system creates an aggregation point to collect, collate, correlate, and fuse information from a variety of sources. However, rather than replacing those sources, it needs all of those security devices, like firewalls, IDS/ IPS, antivirus, anti-spam, and content filters.

Are UTM and SIEM both required?

UTM and SIEM perform their tasks in different ways. SIEM systems work to integrate the efforts of all other security devices. While SIEM's functionality cannot be replaced, it can be done away with for very small organizations with a limited number of security devices, no difficulty in handling/managing security devices separately, and easy, consolidated control and reporting.

While UTM replaces firewalls, IDS/IPS, antivirus/anti-spam, and content filtering devices, it cannot replace SIEM. Rather, SIEM can utilize UTM's input for better control and reporting.

Therefore, UTM and SIEM can both be employed, and together can form a comprehensive defensive suite against IT threats.

Conclusion

The importance of computer and network security is growing day by day. With the boom of information technology in general, and increasing information security needs in particular, no one should stay ignorant of computer system and network security.

It is up to top management to determine the security needs of an organization's physical assets, computer/network systems, and other information technology (IT). But top managers, in many cases, find it too difficult to understand the technology and, therefore, they delegate this responsibility to only the IT department. Even routine security requirements are often considered too technical by many executives, who leave the issues for the information security experts alone to resolve.

It is imperative to understand that technology or an IT department alone cannot make systems secure. Security mechanisms emanate from general security policies formulated by senior management; they are not simply technical issues for the IT department to handle. In order to create a comprehensive information security policy, fundamental knowledge of information security goals and technologies should also be considered.

This book was written to provide an overview and brief description of the fundamental aspects of computer and network security. After reading this book, top managers should be less hesitant about information security decision-making and more willing to discuss intricate information security matters with technical experts.

About the Author

A well-known and respected member of the Information Technology industry, Abdul B. Subhani is an angel investor, entrepreneur, and public speaker. Abdul was born in Multan and raised in Islamabad, Pakistan. He came to the United States in 1998. He is the founder and President/CEO of Centex Technologies, an IT consulting company with offices in Central Texas, Dallas, and Atlanta.

Since, 2002 he has been an adjunct faculty member of Computer Information Technology and Systems - Distance Learning Department & Continuing Education Department of Central Texas College. He has developed computer courses for the Central Texas College Continuing Education Department, and he has written two books: one on Microsoft Outlook, published by Central Texas College, and *Intro to WWW Marketing*, published by Abbott Press. Abdul is also a current adjunct faculty member of the Texas A&M University - Central Texas Computer Information Systems Department.

Abdul has a bachelor's degree in Computer Technology and a master's degree in Information Systems. In addition to his degrees, Abdul has earned multiple advanced credentials, including Microsoft Certified Systems Engineer, Certified Ethical Hacker, Certified Fraud Examiner, Certified in Risk and Information Systems Control, Certified Internal Controls Auditor, Certified Internet Marketer, Certified Anti-Terrorism Specialist, Texas Licensed – Private Investigator, Certified Project Manager E-Business, Certified E-Commerce Consultant and CompTIA Network+, and Security+.

Abdul has used his experience working with technology gurus, business owners, and more to speak at conferences around the country. He has been a frequent keynote speaker, moderator, and panelist at leading international technology conferences, and he has given speeches to thousands of students at colleges and universities.

Abdul is actively involved in his community as a member of Exchange Club, former chairman of Boys & Girls Clubs of Central Texas corporate board, vice chairman of the Killeen Chamber of Commerce, a board member of Central Texas College Foundation, a board member of the Killeen Independent School District Education Foundation, chair of Technology Committee – Career Center of Killeen Independent School District, and a board member of the Texas A&M University – Central Texas Foundation and Alumni Association.